I Kn❤w That I Kn❤w

THE CERTAINTY OF CHRISTIAN FAITH

Jacob Behnken

NORTHWESTERN PUBLISHING HOUSE
Milwaukee, Wisconsin

Northwestern Publishing House
N16W23379 Stone Ridge Dr., Waukesha WI 53188-1108
www.nph.net
© 2020 by Northwestern Publishing House
Published 2020
Printed in the United States of America
ISBN 978-0-8100-2957-6
ISBN 978-0-8100-2958-3 (e-book)

22 23 24 25 26 27 28 29   10 9 8 7 6 5 4 3 2

Contents

Preface

Where do we come from? What does life mean? Where are we going? In one way or another, every human being seeks answers to such questions. Sometimes people look for the answers deliberately. Others stumble through life with default answers impressed upon them by outside influences. In the end, however, everyone believes something. Everybody has a confession of faith. Why do we care about such questions? Ultimately, it's because we need the answer to satisfy the concern that burns in every one of our souls: Am I on the right path? What will happen to me after I die? What must I do to be saved?

Human beings have arrived at many different answers. Throughout history, many societies have devised elaborate religious systems in their attempts to find them. In spite of all their unique characteristics, all of these answers share a common thread. All of them in one way or another prescribe a life of virtue with the end goal of earning and obtaining one's salvation. "Do this! Don't do that!" If people can follow the rules to an acceptable degree, they can hope to receive good from whatever their conception of the divine happens to be.

In more recent times, human wisdom has turned to rejecting theistic views. It denies any kind of god and prefers material explanations for everything. Indeed, modern wisdom denies the existence of anything beyond that which is observable, and as a result, teaches that *being saved* is freeing oneself from the outdated modes of living of past generations in order to find happiness in whatever pleases the individual or perhaps works for the good of society during our finite (and ultimately meaningless) existence. Even a worldview like this, however, is in the end seeking an answer to the same age-old question: "What must I do to be saved?" Though the particulars differ from one worldview to another, a common thread remains constant; being saved involves doing something, the right thing, whatever that may be.

In a world that teaches that salvation is ultimately a function of our own actions, Christianity stands apart. "What must I do to be saved?" The Christian faith answers that question not as a matter of doing but as a matter of believing. "Believe in the Lord Jesus, and you will be saved" (Acts 16:31).

The Christian faith proclaims that salvation doesn't depend on us at all. God sent his Son. His Son, Jesus Christ, took on human flesh, and he accomplished everything our salvation required. There remains nothing left for us to do, and so God tells us in his Word, "Believe in the Lord Jesus." When we believe in the Lord Jesus, we have the assurance that we will be saved through him and what he has accomplished for us.

Rather than looking inward to try to find answers about our salvation, the Christian finds the answer in God's Word as God has revealed it in Holy Scripture, the divine revelation that testifies to the Savior.

For the conscientious believer, however, that simple statement could raise additional questions: How do I know that I believe? How can I be sure the belief in Jesus that I have is sufficient to reap the saving benefits that God promises me?

The little volume in your hands is intended to provide answers to those questions. Together we will turn to God's Word, and through it, we will seek to define saving faith and to see how believers can be sure that we have it—so that we can say, "I know that I know."

As we turn to what God's Word says, we'll find that our gracious God gives us certainty in our faith so that we can have the peace of assurance in our salvation. In our study, we'll find places to apply God's law, his will for us to carry out. That law gives us appropriate warnings when we find ourselves in moments of spiritual apathy or laziness. More than that, however, we'll find opportunities to apply God's gospel, his good news. That gospel serves to give us comfort and peace when we find ourselves recognizing our need for his help and aid. In that way, we'll turn again and again to our Savior Jesus. We'll see that looking to our Savior is ultimately the answer to all of our questions. When we are confronted with that universal question—What must I do to be saved?—may each of us learn to look only and always to Christ, to whom be glory and wisdom and thanks and honor and power and strength forever and ever. ♥

1

I Know That
My Faith Is God's Gift

The man hated Christians. It wasn't simply that he himself didn't believe in Christianity but could respect Christians for their beliefs. No, he was convinced it was the Christian faith that was responsible for his society's problems. If only he could convince more people to agree with him, to see the light of reason like he did, then he was sure more would renounce Christ like he did.

This man's sentiments were not simply idealistic musings. He put his beliefs into action. He did everything he could to stamp out Christianity everywhere he went. In fact, he traveled from place to place bent on putting an end to this faith. If he couldn't convince Christianity's followers with reason, then he would compel them with threats of prison—or worse. This man was the archenemy and persecutor of any and all who confessed Jesus of Nazareth as their Savior.

Then one day everything changed. He was traveling a considerable distance to another community to continue his mission of destruction when he met someone along the way. A light flashed around him, and a voice thundered from heaven, "Saul, Saul, why do you persecute me?" (Acts 9:4). Imagine the sinking feeling this man Saul must have felt. He had carried out his tasks of terror with such confidence. He was certain he was doing the right thing, and in an instant, all that self-assurance must have vanished. Saul had not only been persecuting helpless men, women, and children for whom the law of the land provided no recourse. No, he was persecuting one powerful enough to bring Saul to his knees in seconds, one who could raise a thunderous voice and flash a blinding light from above.

If only to confirm what he might have already deduced, Saul had a question: "Who are you, Lord?" That title of respect didn't yet reflect a faith in the one speaking; it was an acknowledgment that the one speaking occupied a higher position than Saul as he lay there on the ground. "I am Jesus, whom you are persecuting," came the answer (Acts 9:5).

No doubt this answer represented Saul's worst fears realized. All this work he had carried out with such enthusiasm to destroy the fledgling Christian church had been all wrong. All those people he had thrown into prison hadn't been wrong. He was. Saul heard this shocking revelation and witnessed the flashing light, but when he stood up, he was blind. Physical blindness illustrated what was true on a spiritual level for Saul all along. He could not and had not seen the truth.

In this way began one of the most remarkable and significant transformations in Christian history. From sworn enemy of the Christian church came the gospel's great champion who would carry the good news of Jesus throughout the Roman Empire. The church, therefore, remembers this Pharisee named Saul on his way to Damascus that day as the apostle Paul who would bring the gospel to the gentile nations.

Why would God choose such a one to proclaim his Word? We can't claim to understand every reason God may have for carrying out his will in certain ways. What we can say with certainty is what he tells us in his inspired Scripture.

Shortly after the tumultuous events Saul experienced on the road to Damascus, the Lord sent another Christian, a man named Ananias, to restore Saul's sight and his spirit. Ananias didn't warm immediately to his assignment. Saul's reputation had preceded him, and Ananias didn't think marching into his presence and proclaiming his Christian faith was such a good idea, but the Lord insisted. "Go! This man is my chosen instrument to proclaim my name to the Gentiles and their kings and to the people of Israel. I will show him how much he must suffer for my name" (Acts 9:15,16).

We could surmise several reasons why Paul was an ideal choice to carry the Lord's gospel to the Gentiles. He had received a superb education in the ways of Judaism as a Pharisee (the strictest sect of Judaism). That education would have well prepared him to point the Jews to Christ as the fulfillment of the Old Testament faith and Scripture. Paul also was well-acquainted with the wisdom and learning of the Greco-Roman world, which made him an ideal choice to share Christ with those steeped in that worldview. Paul, moreover, was born into the empire as a Roman citizen, a lofty status that granted him special rights and privileges during his travels. We see Paul, in fact, making wise use of his Roman citizenship several times during his ministry. In retrospect, we can see the Lord's wisdom in choosing Paul, this most unlikely candidate for gospel ministry, as his chosen instrument to become the foremost spokesperson for the gospel not only in the New Testament church's early days but in its entire history.

But the Lord wasn't only interested in Paul's unique skill set and how he could put it to use in gospel ministry; he was also interested in Paul on an individual level. Notice how the Lord saw serving in the ministry as an opportunity for Paul to grow in his own faith too. "I will show him how much he must suffer for my name" (Acts 9:16), he explained to Ananias. The Lord had a lesson for the great persecutor of his church. As an apostle sent out by the Lord, Paul would find himself on the receiving end of the persecution he had once doled out to others. He himself would suffer for Jesus' name, as he himself had inflicted sufferings on Christ's people.

The Lord wasn't taking revenge on Paul. This wasn't divine retribution. If it had been, then Paul deserved far worse both in time and in eternity. No, the Lord had only loving discipline in mind for this child of his whom he had designated his spokesperson. Through the sufferings Paul faced, he would learn to put his faith and trust in the Lord and not in himself. He would learn to know Christ's love even in the face of suffering. He would learn his strength came not from human power or wisdom but from the Lord who gives every good and gracious gift from above.

For centuries, the Christian church has praised God for the unique blessings he has brought on his church through the work and writings of the apostle Paul. Of all those Jesus sent out with the good news, we remember Paul as "the apostle" for good reason. With even greater zeal than he showed in persecuting the church, he worked to bring Jesus to every corner of the Mediterranean world. Through Paul, the Lord built his church in community after community. Through Paul, Jews and Gentiles alike came to know the Savior whom God had promised to all people from the beginning. Yes, it was through Paul that God would in large part bring fulfillment to the promise he had made seven hundred years before through Isaiah: "Arise, shine, for your light has come, and the glory of the LORD rises upon you. See, darkness covers the earth and thick darkness is over the peoples, but the LORD rises upon you and his glory appears over you. Nations will come to your light, and kings to the brightness of your dawn" (60:1-3).

Paul could see and give thanks for how the Lord was accomplishing great things through him, but it's noteworthy that for all he could have attributed to himself in sinful pride, he always gave credit where credit was due. He recognized that he owed the success of his ministry to the Lord. That's why he told the Romans, "I will not venture to speak of anything except what Christ has accomplished through me in leading the Gentiles to obey God by what I have said and done—by the power of signs and wonders, through the power of the Spirit of God" (15:18,19).

Not only did Paul attribute his success to the Lord, but he recognized everything he was and did as a Christian he owed to his gracious God. Consider the humility he demonstrated as he spoke to the young pastor Timothy who was following in his footsteps: "I thank Christ Jesus our Lord, who has given me strength, that he considered me trustworthy, appointing me to his service. Even though I was once a blasphemer and a persecutor and a violent man, I was shown mercy because I acted in ignorance and unbelief. The grace of our Lord was poured out on me abundantly, along with the faith and love that are in Christ Jesus. Here is a trustworthy saying that deserves full acceptance: Christ Jesus came into the world to save sinners— of whom I am the worst. But for that very reason I was shown mercy so that in me, the worst of sinners, Christ Jesus might display his immense patience as an example for those who would believe in him and receive eternal life" (1 Timothy 1:12-16).

Paul recognized he did not deserve to serve in the Lord's church. He, moreover, recognized he didn't deserve to belong to God's church at all. All of it was a gift of God. So when Paul wrote to the Ephesians about faith, he wasn't speaking in the abstract. He wasn't talking to them as "others" who needed God to awaken them from their spiritual death and give them new life, while he himself existed on some higher spiritual plane. No, Paul was including himself as he explained that a right relationship with God is always and entirely a gift of grace from God's hand.

God's plan to save

"As for you," Paul wrote, "you were dead in your transgressions and sins" (Ephesians 2:1). Death means the absence of life. Being in the state of death from a spiritual standpoint means we have no spiritual life in us and, as a result, no ability in ourselves to approach God by our own power. No more than a corpse could stand up from the morgue's table and grasp something in its hand could human beings in their natural state of spiritual death reach out to God. Why not? Because they're dead. That, Paul recognized, was his own state and the state of every other man, woman, and child ever to inhabit the earth before the Lord came to them.

That means if something in that dead, natural state is going to change, then God alone is the one to make it happen. Paul shared the good news with the Ephesians and with all the world: "Because of his great love for us, God, who is rich in mercy, made us alive with Christ even when we were dead in transgressions—it is by grace you have been saved. And God raised us up with Christ and seated us with him in the heavenly realms in Christ Jesus, in order that in the coming ages he might show the incomparable riches of his grace, expressed in his kindness to us in Christ Jesus. For it is by grace you have been saved, through faith—and this is not from yourselves, it is the gift of God—not by works, so that no one can boast" (Ephesians 2:4-9).

God made us alive. When we were dead, he gave us life. Paul tells us how. Its basis is what a man named Jesus did for us. This Jesus was no ordinary man. He entered this world in an extraordinary way. Not with a human father and mother but as the Son of God himself, Jesus was conceived by the Holy Spirit of God in the womb of a virgin named Mary. As the Son of God, Jesus did not enter the world with the stain of sin that every other man, woman, and child has carried as an inheritance from their sinful parents. Unlike any other human being, Jesus could and did fulfill God's law perfectly without even the slightest failure. He offered his perfect life as the payment price for the sin of the world on a cross where he bled and died. In that sacrifice, the penalty for sin was paid in full with the precious blood of God's own Son (Acts 20:28). As a result, death could no longer hold Jesus, and he rose from the dead on the third day as the victor in the battle against sin, death, and the devil.

With the work of Jesus, God has reconciled the world to himself (2 Corinthians 5:19). Though sin still plagues us on this earth, Christ has atoned for sin. He has taken away its curse and punishment. Yes, Christ has accomplished everything to save us. As he hung on the cross before he died, he proclaimed in a loud voice, "It is finished" (John 19:30). What was finished was the work necessary to save us from our sin. Jesus had lived the perfect life. He had died the death the sin of the world deserved. He had done everything. As a result, it was (and is) finished.

Paul tells us that these great blessings become ours through faith. Through faith God distributes to individual sinners the blessings Christ has won through his life, death, and resurrection.

Faith's role

What is faith? What does it look like? How marvelous that the one whom God used to reveal these truths to us also serves as a living, breathing example of those truths. As Paul's life illustrates, faith is a gift from God. We do nothing to earn or deserve it. We cannot produce or create it. Instead, it is a gift of God through which we believe and trust in his words and promises. At the end of Mark's gospel, Jesus told his disciples, "Whoever believes and is baptized will be saved, but whoever does not believe will be condemned" (Mark 16:16). Jesus has accomplished everything to save us. Nothing remains for us to do, and so he tells us simply to believe, and everything he has won for us is ours. We receive the benefits of Christ's completed work through faith.

Faith is belief. It is believing what Jesus says is true and trusting that what he says applies to me. Without faith, no one is saved. In other words, if someone does not believe, then that person has forfeited the benefits of the saving work Jesus has accomplished for him or her. Such a person will stand before God not on the basis of Christ's perfect life and sacrifice for him or her (though it was certainly for that person) but on the basis of his or her own merit. Sadly, because all humankind is lost in sin (Psalm 14:3), such a one will have no hope. Unbelievers will be lost, condemned for their sin for all eternity.

For the person with faith in Jesus, however, God credits the merit of Christ's saving work as a gift. Such a person still has sin. It is true, therefore, that left to themselves, those with faith would be just as guilty as the unbeliever. Because of God's undeserved love, however, as we look to him through faith, God regards believers as having the righteousness Christ lived in our place. Paul describes this wondrous grace in his letter to the Romans. He says, "Now to the one who works, wages are not credited as a gift but as an obligation. However, to the one who does not work but trusts God who justifies the ungodly, their faith is credited as righteousness" (Romans 4:4,5). Though we are indeed wicked because of our sin, God considers us righteous through our faith in Jesus who was righteous in our place. What grace! What undeserved love!

So how do we get that faith? Is our believing in Jesus our contribution (however small) to the equation of being saved?

To understand how God's Word answers these questions, we must keep in mind what Scripture has revealed is true about us. Remember, by nature we are dead in sin. We cannot make any move toward God, including making a decision to have faith. The apostle Paul made that clear to the Corinthians when he wrote, "No one can say, 'Jesus is Lord,' except by the Holy Spirit" (1 Corinthians 12:3). It is only the work of God the Holy Spirit himself who enables us to make a confession of faith. Looking at it another way, Paul told the Romans, "The mind governed by the flesh is hostile to God; it does not submit to God's law, nor can it do so" (Romans 8:7). In our sin, we do not believe or trust in God as he would have us do. Instead, we are hostile to him. We are his enemies. Note, in fact, that not even the ability to change that status is within us: we *cannot* do what we ought to do. Faith, therefore, cannot be our contribution to our salvation. It cannot be the part we play in God's plan to save us from sin.

God is clear about where faith comes from. In the same chapter where Paul tells us we were dead in our sin and that we are saved by God's grace, he also tells us about faith, "It is by grace you have been saved, through faith—and this not from yourselves, it is the gift of God" (Ephesians 2:8). Yes, our faith is a gift from God. Only he can give it to the sinner who would otherwise have no hope.

As Jesus' listeners grumbled that his teachings were too hard to accept, he rebuked them as he made the observation,

"No one can come to me unless the Father who sent me draws them" (John 6:44). Yes, it is God who must take action if we are going to believe in him, and by his grace, that's exactly what he does. The fact we or anyone is saved is a gift from God from start to finish.

Paul himself—through whom God revealed these truths clearly—was a living, breathing proof of his own teaching. He was on the road to Damascus bent on destroying Christ and those who would dare confess his name. Sadly, he was on another road too. Like all humankind without the Savior, he was on the road to hell and eternal condemnation. But God in his grace intervened. In a miraculous and powerful way, God pulled him off that road to hell and gave him faith so that the same Jesus he had previously spoken murderous threats against he now confessed as his Lord and Savior. This name of Jesus he previously had wanted to rid from the earth he carried from nation to nation. Yes, God would use for his saving purpose the mouth that once breathed out threats against Christ's people and the hands that once threw Christians into dungeons. Paul would serve as God's instrument to carry Jesus to the world. Paul, the one-time persecutor of Christ, could now confess, "Although I am less than the least of all the Lord's people, this grace was given me: to preach to the Gentiles the boundless riches of Christ, and to make plain to everyone the administration of this mystery, which for ages past was kept hidden in God, who created all things" (Ephesians 3:8,9). It was an undeserved gift of God's grace for him to have the privilege of speaking God's Word to the world.

But even more foundational than that, it was a gift of God's grace for Paul to know and believe in Christ as his own Savior from all his sins, even his sins of persecuting Christ and his church. It's important to remember that in spite of Paul's excellent earthly education and pedigree, it was none of those things that enabled Paul to believe. (In fact, consider how all of that—without the intervention of the Holy Spirit—had led him down the wrong path!) None of it enabled Paul to discover the truth for himself. If he had relied on his own intellect, he would have gone on regarding the gospel of Christ as foolishness, and dangerous foolishness at that. Instead, for Paul to have faith it was necessary for the Lord to call him in a miraculous way.

In dramatic fashion, the Lord Jesus forced Paul to see his own sin and evil. All the time Paul thought he was doing God a favor in his persecution of Christianity, he was, in fact, persecuting the Lord of heaven and earth. All the time Paul believed his life was earning merit and God's favor, he was, in fact, insulting the Lord with an imperfect and unsatisfactory kind of obedience. After that dramatic experience on the road to Damascus, the Lord had Paul sit and wait in the city to find out what would happen next. No doubt during those three days, Paul considered how much he had gotten it all wrong. Perhaps he even prayed words like the ones from Psalm 130, "Out of the depths I cry to you, LORD" (verse 1). For the first time, the reality of Paul's sin and inadequacy confronted him head-on. The Lord confronted Paul and brought him to repentance, a work only he can accomplish in human hearts.

Yes, God was and is gracious and compassionate. Though Paul certainly didn't deserve it, God had grace and forgiveness in abundance for him. Yes, the law's sting was preparatory to what would come next. Through his servant Ananias, God assured Paul his sin was taken away. "As far as the east is from the west, so far has he removed our transgressions from us" (Psalm 103:12). God gave Paul that personal assurance. He blessed him with faith in his Savior. Could it be any clearer? Paul's faith was a gift from God through and through.

Maybe your coming to faith wasn't visibly as miraculous. Maybe it didn't include three days of waiting for the conclusion to the story. Maybe you can't even personally recall the particular event when it happened, but the truth is no different when it comes to your faith. It was just as much of a miracle for you as it was for Paul. It was the same gift God gave to that wayward Pharisee. When you confess Christ as your Savior, you can be sure. To you, God has given the gift of faith.

That's important to understand about faith. Faith is not something we conjure up in ourselves. It's not something we have because we are naturally more enlightened than others around us, nor is it the result of human learning or wisdom. We weren't able to make a decision and welcome Christ into our hearts. We didn't have the ability to do any of those things. We were dead in our transgressions and sins.

But God himself came to you. Perhaps he did that long before you can even remember. Perhaps it took place at a font in a church somewhere when a pastor applied water and said, "I baptize you in the name of the Father and of the Son and of the Holy Spirit." In that water, God saved you "through the washing of rebirth and renewal by the Holy Spirit, whom he poured out on us generously through Jesus Christ our Savior" (Titus 3:5,6). Through the gift of faith God gave you there, he gave you rebirth and new life.

Perhaps for some it took place through a caring Christian friend speaking the good news to them. To them (and all Christians) Peter says, "You have been born again, not of perishable seed, but of imperishable, through the living and enduring word of God" (1 Peter 1:23).

As much as it was impossible for us to contribute to our own physical conception and birth, so it is the work of another we are born again spiritually. It was the work of God, and he accomplishes it by blessing us with his gift of faith, a gift that he worked in us by the power of the good news of Jesus (Romans 1:16).

So as you think about your own faith, always remember that it is something precious God has given you. Left to yourself, you could have never hoped to attain it. It was never something you could have come up with on your own. That's an incredibly humbling thought for human beings who always want to be self-sufficient.

At the same time, it's an incredibly comforting thought too. God loved you so much that he not only sent his Son to die for you, but he even worked in you the gift of faith so that you could believe it, all while you were far from him in unbelief. In faith, God has given each of us an unearned and undeserved gift, and a priceless one at that!

As we consider several different aspects of our faith in the upcoming chapters, think of it like gazing at a multifaceted jewel. As we can delight in how light reveals a gem's beauty in a myriad of ways as light shines through and reflects off at different angles, so we will behold our faith from several different angles and marvel in the different facets of comfort and assurance it gives us. It does that because it is a precious gift, a gift to us from God. That's why we can know that we know—because our "knowing" is never our work at all. All along, God was and is the one who has given and worked that precious gift within us. ♥

2

I Know That
My Faith Looks to Christ

He was a young man. What could he possibly do in the face of such a problem? Older, more experienced men couldn't even bring themselves to try. They had melted in fear at the very thought of taking action. They cowered like frightened animals as the foe laughed in their faces. Now this young man dared to stand up.

Some of those older men were indignant. Who did this impetuous boy think he was? What gave him the right to be so confident while they were so afraid?

This young man and future king of Israel had an answer for his naysayers: "The LORD who rescued me from the paw of the lion and the paw of the bear will rescue me from the hand of this Philistine" (1 Samuel 17:37).

The young David may have seemed arrogant to his older brothers (and perhaps to others as well) to exude such certainty of success while they could see only defeat. They likely resented the fact he sounded so confident in the face of an enemy like Goliath, even when all the other soldiers of Israel (themselves included) quaked in fear. Who was he to act like that? What made him so bold?

David's brothers could have had a point. If David was simply demonstrating youthful arrogance, if his confidence was in his own skills honed in the shepherd's field against lion and bear, or if he was just trying to show off, then his brothers had every reason to correct him.

The truth, however, was that David's faith rested in none of those things. He could see the towering Goliath's strength and battle-hardened skills as much as anyone else. He recognized his own limitations in the face of an enemy like that. But David's faith wasn't in himself at all. His faith was in the Lord, the one true God. David trusted the Lord to give him the strength he needed to face his foe and to deliver him in his time of need. David's strength wasn't his confidence itself; his strength was in the One in whom that confidence rested. In that fact lies a key truth about faith.

Faith's source of strength

In a general sense, human society may approve of faith. In many contexts, faith can serve as a sort of quasi-religious concept that no one will take issue or be uncomfortable with. Even an unbeliever might encourage someone else to "have faith" in the face of trouble or difficulty. Without defining faith any further than a general kind of hope or good feeling, everyone could agree that faith is a worthy endeavor. "Just have faith that everything will work out" goes a familiar encouragement. People with faith, after all, will be positive-thinking. They won't be as easily shaken as the person without any kind of faith at all because they'll have some optimism for the future in the face of the individual events of life, even if those events are sometimes tragic.

Likewise, all people, whether they realize it or not, hold to one kind of faith or another. Some have an enduring faith in themselves. They have self-confidence and believe if they put their mind to something, they can achieve anything. Some have faith in society. They believe that the human race is on a constant path of improvement and that we can ultimately trust the masses to do the right things. Many today have faith in science. If they read an assertion in a science book or academic journal, then they accept it without any further consideration. Though many today might reject the moniker of being religious, they still might have faith in some kind of cosmic fate. "All things are working together toward a unified and purpose-driven end," they might believe. One could argue that human beings are wired to have faith. The objects of faith might be as diverse as the people who hold to them but, still, we all have faith.

That's why it's essential to understand the difference between faith in a general sense and true Christian faith. The difference lies in the fact that the Christian faith has a definite object. The Christian faith has value not simply because it is a virtuous trait of the one practicing it but because it rests in a definite object, in a definite someone.

Imagine someone is drowning at sea. A rescue boat speeds to save the victim, and the rescue worker in the boat throws out a life ring. He shouts to the one bobbing up and down in the water, "Grab hold!" Of course the drowning individual does so. The life ring keeps him afloat, and the rescuer pulls him to safety.

Consider for a moment how it really wasn't the man's faith in the life ring that saved him. It's true that if he had rejected the life ring and said, "I want nothing to do with a silly thing like that," he would have drowned. A lack of faith could have doomed him, but even so, it wasn't the virtue of faith within the man that brought about his rescue. No, it was the life ring itself with its buoyancy on the water, its handles to grab hold of, and the rope that connected it to the boat. The life ring did the saving.

Imagine if instead the rescuer had some kind of sick sense of humor and threw out the boat's anchor instead of a flotation device and yet still called, "Grab hold!" The man in his desperation could have trusted the instructions and said, "Well, this rescuer must know what he's doing." His faith could have been just as strong in that scenario, but nevertheless an anchor would only speed his sinking into the depths. The object of one's faith matters.

The people of this world can have faith in many different kinds of anchors too. It might feel like a virtuous quality to have.

The objects of their faith might make them feel good too, but in the end, an anchor does not keep a person afloat the howling winds and crashing waves.

The Bible does also speak of faith in a certain sense as a virtue. It is a fruit that enables us to believe and trust in the words and promises of God. The apostle Paul, in fact, mentions it in his list of the fruits of the Spirit in his letter to the Galatians: "The fruit of the Spirit is love, joy, peace, forbearance, kindness, goodness, *faithfulness*, gentleness and self-control" (5:22,23). The English word *faithfulness* in this verse is, in fact, a translation of the same Greek word that English Bibles often render simply as "faith."

On the one hand, all Christians have faith in the sense that the definition of a Christian is one who has faith in the Lord Jesus as Savior (Acts 16:31). As a fruit of the Spirit, however, it's also true that different Christians have different measures of it as a particular fruit. The first letter to the Corinthians describes this reality: "Now to each one the manifestation of the Spirit is given for the common good. To one there is given through the Spirit a message of wisdom, to another a message of knowledge by means of the same Spirit, to another faith by the same Spirit, to another gifts of healing by that one Spirit, to another miraculous powers, to another prophecy, to another distinguishing between spirits, to another speaking in different kinds of tongues, and to still another the interpretation of tongues. All these are the work of one and the same Spirit, and he distributes them to each one, just as he determines" (1 Corinthians 12:7-11). Notice how just as the Holy Spirit distributes a variety of spiritual gifts in different measures to different Christians, so the Holy Spirit blesses Christians with different measures of faith. Yes, all believers by definition have faith in Jesus. No, not every believer will have the same strength and measure of faith.

Some Christians will exhibit a rock-solid faith, no matter what they may face in life. Think of Shadrach, Meshach, and Abednego who, in defiance against the world's most powerful king and in the face of near-certain death, refused to bow down to an idol and remained faithful to the Lord their God (Daniel 3). Think of Peter and John who, against the authority of the people's own religious leaders, when told to stop preaching in Jesus' name, declared, "We cannot help speaking about what we have seen and heard" (Acts 4:20). Think of people in our own lives who demonstrate a faith in the Lord that we consider remarkable, especially when we reflect on what they may have endured in life.

Some believers, on the other hand, may have a weaker faith. Doubts and questions may plague them to a higher degree than they do for other Christians. Perhaps in their walk of faith they will more often depend on the help and encouragement of other Christians.

The Lord, in fact, has special comfort for those people struggling with weakness of faith. For the troubled in faith, the Lord assures us how he regards the weak. The prophet Isaiah says, "A bruised reed [the Lord] will not break, and a smoldering wick he will not snuff out" (42:3). No, the Lord doesn't cast away from his presence those whose faith is weak or faltering. Instead, he assures them that he shows special care and even affection for them. He doesn't snuff out the light of their faith. He doesn't break them off from his people because their connection with him is bruised. He deals with them gently and tenderly. He does it because he loves his people.

Of course, at different points in their lives the same Christians may exhibit either a stronger or a weaker faith. Remember how on the night of Jesus' death, Peter had quaked with fear and denied with curses that he even knew Jesus. He had put his own life and safety ahead of the truth and ahead of his Savior and friend. Peter's denial had brought him great shame. When Jesus caught his eye in that courtyard, Peter remembered that his friend and Lord had warned him that he would deny him, and yet still he had fallen. How weak Peter's faith was in those moments! But the Lord in his grace restored Peter. After Jesus' resurrection, he appeared to Peter alone (1 Corinthians 15:5). He gently restored him and assured him he was still one of his

17

chosen apostles (John 21:15-20). That restoration allowed Peter, who was once so weak in faith, to become that great apostle of faith. Soon he would be that bold ambassador for Christ who defied the wishes of the powerful Sanhedrin and insisted on speaking about what he had seen and heard. How great Peter's faith had become!

Likewise, faith may vary in its level of knowledge and understanding. Some Christians may enjoy a vast knowledge of God's Word and have a grasp of all the various teachings in it. Perhaps that knowledge enables them to grasp the details of Scripture's teaching with clarity and accuracy and to instruct other believers who do not have the same level of knowledge.

Another believer's faith may be adorned with less knowledge. Consider the faith of those with some kind of mental impairment. They know their Savior Jesus, but they may never be able to explain or even understand much of Scripture's teaching. Is such faith any less saving? Of course not! Though their faith may be below average in terms of knowledge, it may, as is so often the case, excel in its trust and readiness to believe. Regardless of the particular qualities of a believer's faith, faith makes all believers into dear children of God. Through faith, God credits believers with their Savior's perfect righteousness in their place.

We might also consider the faith of young children or infants. Can little children have faith? Can they believe? Even when Jesus' own disciples thought that children would waste his precious time, the Savior's own words take as a given that his little ones can and do believe. "People were bringing little children to Jesus for him to place his hands on them, but the disciples rebuked them. When Jesus saw this, he was indignant. He said to them, 'Let the little children come to me, and do not hinder them, for the kingdom of God belongs to such as these. Truly I tell you, anyone who will not receive the kingdom of God like a little child will never enter it.' And he took the children in his arms, placed his hands on them and blessed them" (Mark 10:13-16).

Yes, Jesus tells us in plain language that little children can believe. In fact, he holds up little children as a model of faith for other believers to emulate. Spending some time with little children tells us why. Little children have great trust, especially when it comes to those they love.

Jesus' encouragement to believe like little children teaches us a great deal about faith. Faith is not simply knowledge of the mind. Faith is also trust; it is the trust that what God says in his Word applies to us. Even when we might wonder how a little child or even an infant can have the knowledge necessary to have faith, we can recognize that these little ones certainly love and trust. Think of the newborn who cries in the arms of others but immediately finds peace in the arms of his mother, as he hears her soothing voice. That infant might not have knowledge of his mother in the way adults usually think of knowledge, but nevertheless, he knows her in a way that passes our understanding. So too Jesus teaches us that little ones know and believe in their dear heavenly Father.

So to the weak in faith and to those whose are more simple in faith, Jesus gives the assurance that he is theirs and they are his. That's certainly true because they enjoy the blessings he has won for them with his life and death. And how can they be certain? Again, remember that the saving aspect of faith is not the virtuous character of faith. Rather, faith saves because of its object. That object is Christ our Savior himself.

Even Jesus' disciples needed a lesson on faith from time to time. On one occasion, after Jesus had finished teaching a lesson on forgiveness, the disciples thought they needed more faith. Who could blame them? They probably heard Jesus' words about how his followers are to be ready to forgive again and again, and they concluded, "Who is up to such a task? How short we have fallen!" They implored Jesus, "Increase our faith!" (Luke 17:5). Jesus had an unexpected response to the disciples' request. He told them, "If you have faith as small as a mustard seed, you can say to this mulberry tree, 'Be uprooted and planted in the sea,' and it will obey you" (Luke 17:6).

19

The disciples had it all wrong. They were looking for the strength of their faith in themselves and their own ability. They thought they needed a greater faith so that they would have the ability to do what Jesus commanded. The disciples, however, were looking for their faith's strength in the wrong place. Faith is a powerful thing not in its own right. Its power rests in the object of that faith: in Christ. Even faith as small as a mustard seed could produce an unimaginable miracle. But how? Because faith gets its strength from its object, from Christ.

Think back to the life ring. Why does it save? It saves because of its buoyancy in the water. It saves because it displaces enough water so that it does not sink. The result is when someone drowning in the water grabs hold of it, he too stays above water and is saved from a watery demise.

Christ and his cross work the same way. He saves because of his perfect life, his all-atoning sacrifice, and the forgiveness of sins he declared when he said once and for all, "It is finished" (John 19:30). Those who hold on to him through faith are saved in spite of the depths of sin within and around them. Theirs is the gift of forgiveness and eternal life.

Increase my faith!

Of course, no one can deny that a stronger grip on the life ring is preferable. While it doesn't affect the saving quality of the life ring, it certainly makes the whole ordeal of passing through the wind and the waves a little less nerve-wracking. With only a fingertip grip on that ring, any gust of wind, any rush of the waves might cause disaster. It makes both the rescuer and the rescued sweat through every nanosecond until that potential drowning victim is safely in the confines of the rescue ship. That's why a firm grip is far better. With both arms wrapped solidly around the life ring, everyone can breathe a little easier. Could the man lose such a grip? Anything is possible, but that firm grip diminishes the risk. Sure, the wind might pound on him. Certainly the waves will continue to crash over him until the moment he is dragged onto the boat, but with a firm grip, the journey passes with far less fear.

The same is true with faith in Christ. A person with weak faith will be saved for the same reason a person with a strong faith is saved. For this, all praise and glory belongs to Christ! And yet, a weak faith can make us nervous. The wind and waves of this life—trouble, hardship, persecution, hunger, disease, pain—are all things Satan can and does use in trying to get us to lose our grip. Sadly, sometimes he succeeds. That's why a strong faith is a wonderful blessing from the Lord. Against such a faith, the wind and waves of this life can beat, but the strength of that faith will make it far less susceptible to the devil's attacks. Yes, a strong faith is a blessing indeed.

Yet even as we praise God for the blessing of a strong faith, we remember that its real strength and true power reside in its object, in Christ Jesus, our Savior. Generic faith may have some value on this earth. If someone has "faith" in something that proves reliable, then that person may reap some benefit from it. If, on the other hand, someone's faith was misplaced because the person or thing in whom that faith rests proves unreliable or untrustworthy, then it would have been better for the person not to have faith at all.

In contrast to all other faiths, however, faith in Christ and his Word is always a sure and certain thing. It is sure and certain because its object is unshakable and unchangeable. His promises are always sure. He never reneges on his Word. He is the solid rock. When people build their faith on him, then the storm can come, but they will find a sure and certain foundation.

Building a house takes planning. A good builder will have detailed blueprints that capture all the different aspects of a project—the structural supports, the plumbing, the electrical, the heating and cooling ducts. None of that matters, however, if the foundation isn't right. A builder could construct the most beautiful, most impressive house with all the latest styles, but if that house rests on a bed of quicksand, none of that fine construction work will last for long. On the other hand, even the most modest shack can endure for year after year if the builder made sure to construct it on a rock-solid foundation.

Jesus likened the walk of faith to the work of a builder. In one of his parables he told the crowds, "Therefore everyone who hears these words of mine and puts them into practice is like a wise man who built his house on the rock. The rain came down, the streams rose, and the winds blew and beat against that house; yet it did not fall, because it had its foundation on the rock. But everyone who hears these words of mine and does not put them into practice is like a foolish man who built his house on sand. The rain came down, the streams rose, and the winds blew and beat against that house, and it fell with a great crash" (Matthew 7:24-27).

So when faith is strong or when faith is weak, where do we look? When we consider our own faith and wonder how we can be sure it is saving, where do we find comfort? When we wonder how the simple faith of a tiny child who lacks so much in the way of knowledge can really be faith, what is the solution? The answer is always the same. Faith saves because of its object. We look to the rock, to Christ. He is the object of faith. He is the one who does the saving, and faith saves always and only because of him. In a sense, faith forgets about itself because it's occupied on its object.

When you contemplate your own faith, don't spend too much time considering how trusting, how knowledgeable, how patient in trial you are. Instead look to the object of your faith. Look to Christ. Not only does that prevent us from patting ourselves on the back in congratulation when God blesses us with a strong faith, but it also keeps our hearts from despair when we find the strength of our faith is far from ideal.

In strength of faith, we give thanks to Christ for his gracious gift, and we remember that every spiritual blessing we owe to him. In weakness of faith, we look to him for strength and trust that even when our hearts fail, nothing can pluck us from his hand—because he is our rock. ♥

3

I Know That
My Faith Is Certain
of What Is Unseen

The man's beloved son was dying. He had summoned the best doctors and tried the best medicines, but nothing worked. It all seemed to be in vain. It seemed that in this most tragic way, death would have the final say.

The man had only one hope left. He had heard reports of a new rabbi, a teacher. He was teaching a message of authority and was astonishing the crowds before him. As amazing as his teaching was, however, that's not what piqued the man's interest. There were also reports this rabbi was performing miracles, healing people with incurable ailments. He was driving out demons, making the lame to walk, the blind to see, the deaf to hear, and curing people's illnesses, even when all hope seemed lost. Maybe, just maybe, Jesus could do the same thing for his son.

The problem was, Jesus wasn't in the area. If only Jesus was close by, it would have been so much easier. Travel wasn't easy in those days; it involved riding on an animal—if someone was lucky enough to own one—or, more likely, going on foot. This man, however, loved his son; he couldn't bear the thought of losing him, so he resolved to go for it. He would go and see Jesus. It was his last hope to save someone he loved.

God blessed the man's journey. He found Jesus, and even better, Jesus was willing to work the healing the man so desired. There was, however, a catch. Jesus was not going to accompany the man to see his son. Instead, he sent him away with only his word. "Go," Jesus replied, "your son will live" (John 4:50).

Wouldn't it have been normal if the man had expected Jesus to go with him? If Jesus was really going to heal his loved one, couldn't he, shouldn't he have taken the time to go and touch him or put his hands over him? Isn't that how healing someone worked? How would Jesus even know who this boy was he was supposed to heal? Why wouldn't Jesus take the time to make sure? Besides, wouldn't the man have felt better not only if Jesus would see his son in person but if he had Jesus to walk along-side him on the return journey? But no, Jesus only gave him his word, and for that journey home, that's all that man could rely on. And so return he did, armed only with Jesus' promise that when he returned, he would find his son well.

All these centuries later, we have the benefit of knowing the rest of the story from the beginning. We know Jesus was and is the almighty Son of God. He didn't need to be present to bring healing to that sick young man, and of course, Jesus' word accomplished exactly what he promised. There was no need for that man to fear anything less. Jesus' handling of this partic-ular situation in his ministry, however, and the way this man demonstrates his faith are both worthwhile for us to ponder as we consider the nature of faith.

The place of evidence

For so much of what God tells us in his Word, we do not have evidence, at least not to the degree our human natures would prefer. God tells us that in the beginning he created all things. He tells us that he didn't require any building materials. He sim-ply issued forth his almighty Word, and at his command, all creation sprung into being. He tells us that this process didn't require the many eons human logic would imagine it would have taken to complete such an accomplishment. Instead, he tells us that he created all things in the course of six ordinary days. Of course, he could have chosen to devote more time to the task, or he could have created all things in an instant. In his wisdom, however, he chose the same basic work week we use today to carry out our tasks.

For this sublime work of the Almighty we have no direct evidence. The nature of the act itself precludes the possibility of any eyewitness, save the Creator himself. Before anyone or anything had come into being, who could corroborate the first-hand account only God could give? Nor has God seen fit to leave a photo or video record so that mankind of every age can peruse the footage at will.

What's more, human nature is not inclined to believe God, but rather to disbelieve him. This tendency is really no surprise. Since the fall into sin, human nature is not the unbiased arbiter of truth it would like to believe it is, but instead it acts to suppress the truth of God at every turn (Romans 1:18). Any apparent opportunity to discredit God's Word, therefore, will merit the unbelieving world's fanfare and adulation.

So anti-Christian skeptics trot out the geologic record as supposed proof that the world in its current form is the result of the slow forces of nature working over billions of years. Likewise it insists that the fossil record shows how life on our planet has evolved over millions of years from one form of life to another. From the same sources we learn that the petroleum products buried deep in the earth are products of organic material decomposing over a period far longer than a literal reading of God's Word would allow.

Some who still want to believe at least something of God's Word but don't want to appear out of touch with the modern ideas of our age have responded to the pressure of these messages by jettisoning the plain meaning of Scripture as Christians over the centuries have understood it. They suggest God's account of creation in Genesis chapters 1 and 2, for example, is merely a poetic rendering of the reality that modern science explains with greater accuracy. Adherents of such belief want to maintain their Christian faith, but they cannot overcome the allure of an explanation for this vast universe that acknowledges human wisdom and learning.

It's worthwhile to note that apologists for the historic Christian faith can poke plenty of holes in the secular worldview. With some honest introspection, secularists should admit that their own ideas leave many questions unanswered to the inquisitive mind. From where, for example, did the building materials for this vast universe come? How did a chance process like the Big Bang produce a universe with such elegance in structure, complexity, and order? What kind of mathematical odds could randomly produce such a result? How could life spring from the primordial reactions of the early universe and then learn how to reproduce itself so it could improve in a chance process over the eons? Indeed, whenever the secularist suggests that Christians have a difficult time backing up their assertions with evidence, it is worth observing that their worldview requires just as much, if not more, faith to accept.

Likewise, Christians can take comfort in the point that their worldview does much to explain the evidence available to us. An almighty Creator-God with more wisdom and power than our human nature can fathom offers a compelling (yes, the only), reasonable explanation for a universe as vast and complex and perfectly balanced as we observe. The genius of DNA passing on all the instructions to re-create an organism in a single cell offers a beautiful view into the wisdom of the one who commanded his first creatures to "be fruitful and increase in number" (Genesis 1:28). Yes, on both the macro and micro level, this entire creation powerfully "declare[s] the glory of God" in the words of the psalmist (19:1). In this way, God is clearly seen so that unbelievers will be left without any excuse for their refusal to believe (Romans 1:20).

In the end, however, does any of that matter? When we contemplate the nature of faith, we see that faith really does not require evidence at all. On the one hand, it is true that evidence can serve to strengthen and encourage us in our faith. Jesus used the incontrovertible evidence of his resurrection to wipe away the doubts of poor Thomas so that in the face of the evidence he could say nothing other than, "My Lord and my God!" (John 20:28). Likewise, when we consider the compelling evidence for God's Word around us, it can reinforce us in our faith and offer some assurance against the world's challenges to it.

On the other hand, evidence is not a replacement for faith, nor can the evidence in itself create faith. One of the most striking demonstrations of that fact in Scripture comes from the pleadings of a rich man following his death. While he is suffering in hell, he pleads with Abraham to send a poor man named Lazarus who is currently in heaven back to earth to warn his father and brothers of their impending condemnation. He is sure that if Lazarus were to come back from the dead, then his family would recognize the folly of their way and turn to the truth before it was too late for them, as it already was for him. Abraham, however, speaks a remarkable truth. If the rich man's father and brothers would not listen to God's Word spoken through the law and the prophets, they would not believe even if someone would have come back from the dead (Luke 16:31).

When we hear those words, it is easy to doubt the veracity of that claim. "How can that be? If someone were to come back from the dead, I would certainly be more inclined to believe!" That's because we want to believe that we as human beings are neutral. We want to believe that if the proper evidence of something confronts us, then we would be ready and willing to believe whatever is reasonable. The shocking truth Abraham reveals about our human nature, however, is that it is not the case.

Our sinful mind is hostile to God. It does not submit to God's law, nor can it do so (Romans 8:7). Even if we have the right evidence, still that would not be enough to compel us to believe. We find plenty of evidence of that throughout biblical history, especially during Jesus' ministry. Think of all the miracles he performed, wonders that had no explanation except that

27

Jesus was everything he said he was. For example, after Jesus summoned a different man named Lazarus from his grave after he had been there for four days. With the sound of his voice, Jesus raised a man from death. After that, wouldn't one expect that everyone would rush to believe in him? That finally the naysayers would be silenced and everyone would flock to Jesus as the life-giver? Only that's not what happened. Instead we find the exact opposite. Jesus' enemies were enraged. They rushed away from Jesus so that they could plot their next steps. They feared he would cause them to lose their positions of power and prestige, and so they hatched a plan not only to kill Jesus but to kill Lazarus as well, since he was living, breathing proof of who Jesus was and what he could do. Imagine that. Jesus' unbelieving enemies could see the evidence staring them in the face. They could talk to him, and yet that evidence did not create faith in their hearts. It did not lead them to believe. Instead it led to their hardened rejection and unbelief.

On this occasion and in so many others, we find proof of the truth Abraham proclaimed to that rich man suffering in hell. Even if the dead were raised back to life, people would not believe on their own. No, it is not evidence that leads our human hearts to believe.

Instead, as we have seen, faith comes only as a gift of the Holy Spirit, and that gift believes without evidence. The Holy Spirit's gift of faith enables us to trust that which God says. The fact that God said it is evidence enough.

That's why Scripture defines faith in this way: "Faith is confidence in what we hope for and assurance about what we do not see" (Hebrews 11:1). Faith believes what reason cannot comprehend, prove, or understand with logic. Faith allows us to believe what God says in spite of the evidence, in spite of what our reason tells us must be true. When we cannot see the truth, God's gift of faith allows us to believe that truth.

Like a little child

Recall how Jesus praised the faith of little children. Theirs is a faith that all Christians can model. Consider how little children trust. When Mommy or Daddy tells a little child something, there is no doubt. There is no question. There is no second-guessing or need for an explanation. A child accepts what Mommy or Daddy says simply because she knows them, she loves them, and she trusts them. Mommy or Daddy's word is all that is necessary for a little child to believe and accept.

We know that things do not stay this way as children grow and mature. Children learn to think for themselves and apply reason like an adult does. They begin to recognize that their parents are not infallible and can make mistakes. Soon their questions gush out in a flood of words. It begins with an innocent "Why?" But often, a rebellious attitude can soon undergird those questions. The innocent "Why?" morphs into "Why should I do, believe, or listen to what you say anyways? You're not any smarter than I am!" No doubt, such questioning brings pain to parents who hear it, especially as they think back to the little child who was once so accepting of everything Mommy or Daddy said. Parents know too that such rebelliousness comes from a lack of experience and understanding, and so often, this rebellion is going to bring hurt into their children's lives. "If only they would listen and avoid the trouble coming their way," parents think to themselves in anguish.

Recognize the parallel in our relationship with God. The reason Jesus wants us to have faith like a little child is not so that he can dupe us into believing falsehood. It's because he wants what is best for us. When we simply delight to believe and trust what God tells us, then we know we will be on the right path. Our loving God isn't going to lead us astray. He's not manipulative or mean-spirited. When he tells us something, we know he's speaking the truth to us. When he wants us to believe or behave in a certain way, we know he wants to bless us. Unlike earthly parents who can and do make mistakes, God never errs; his Word is flawless (Psalm 12:6).

So like a little child, we can believe, even if we can't understand everything he's telling us, even if we can't see the proof with our own reason or logic, even if everything and everyone else seem to be telling us the opposite. We can strive for confidence in what we hope for and assurance about what we do not see.

We can recognize that reason and logic, and even this world that has fallen into sin can and do lie to us. We know that they are not interested in our eternal welfare and that following them unquestioningly will only result in our death and destruction.

So as we consider our own faith, part of that faith is learning to silence our human reason. That doesn't mean our reason has no use at all. Indeed, God's gift of intelligence and reason serve as one of many proofs that God has made us in a fearful and wonderful way (Psalm 139:14). We can use our reason to comprehend and understand God's creation around us. We can use it to gain insight into God's Word as he reveals it to us (Psalm 119:15). Only we dare not use our reason to question or reject what God has revealed to us in that Word. When we do that, we are abusing the reason God has so graciously given. We are assigning it a task it has no qualification to carry out. Rather than using reason as God intends, as a blessing for us as we go about our earthly lives, we are turning it into a deadly enemy that, given enough time and influence in our lives, will destroy our faith altogether. An important part of our faith, therefore, is learning to use our reason where appropriate and silencing it the moment it would dare stand against its Creator.

That does not mean God is asking us to accept things that are foolish or wrong. His "foolishness" (if there could be such a thing) is wiser than man's wisdom (1 Corinthians 1:25). Thus, because we are limited in our ability to understand, human wisdom will think the truth of what God says is foolish. The reality, however, is always the exact opposite. When human wisdom thinks it knows better than God, in the end, what human wisdom believes is foolishness and what God says remains the truth. God is not like a human being, that he should lie (Numbers 23:19). His Word is the truth (John 17:17). Put another way,

God doesn't ask us to believe things that are irrational. He only asks us to believe things that are super-rational, things that are above and beyond our reason's ability to comprehend.

Learn to accept, yes, to rejoice, in the truth that God is bigger and smarter than you are. Consider opportunities to silence human reason not as a hindrance to your faith but as an exercise of that faith. Faith, after all, is assurance of what we do not see. The church father Anselm of Canterbury put it most beautifully when he said, "I do not seek to understand in order that I may believe, but I believe in order to understand. For this I also believe—that unless I believe I shall not understand."

When we consider the substance of our Christian faith, we find that our God has given us many opportunities to put that proverb into practice. Consider all the things God teaches us that our human reason cannot grasp. God created the world in six days. We cannot explain how that can be. God sent his Son born of a virgin. Nothing in our experience tells us that such a thing could happen. God tells us that this Son rose from the grave. Again, we have no evidence that dead human beings can come back to life, especially after they have been buried or laid in a tomb. God tells us that he uses plain water to wash away sin, and simple bread and wine to give us his body and blood. How can water do such a great thing? How can simple bread and wine offer such a gift in so many different places throughout time? The Lord promises us that he is going to return on the Last Day to judge the living and the dead. He tells us that this world is going to come to an end. Our human observation tells us just the opposite—that this world will keep on turning forever and ever.

Yes, God gives us ample opportunity to silence our human reason and solely trust in him. Don't give in to the temptation to question God even once. When we do that, we set a dangerous pattern for our faith. We are giving a foothold to the devil who will certainly use that foothold to gain even greater gains for himself. We are leaving a vulnerability in our spiritual armor that exposes us to deadly injury.

Instead, rely on the plain and simple Word of God—all of it. Like that man with the sick son, go on your journey of life armed with Jesus' promise. It may have seemed like a flimsy thing for the man to put all his hope in as he returned to his home. How could Jesus promise healing like that? How could he do such a thing from so far away, especially in a matter so important to that man? But Jesus, of course, didn't let that man down. When he did walk through the door of his house, he found his son well. Jesus had done exactly as he promised.

Jesus promises the same to you. Your faith can always trust his Word, even if you can't always see how it can be so. Like that man, like your fellow believers throughout the ages, your faith gives you the blessing of being certain of that which is not seen. ♥

4

I Know That
My Faith Bears Fruit

God had accomplished something amazing. In a city without enough God-fearing people even to construct a synagogue, the Lord had built up his church to the extent that this local congregation was taking an active role in spreading the gospel to new communities. Yes, the Christian congregation in Philippi had grown in unlikely circumstances and to an unexpected extent.

Paul and his coworker Silas had arrived in Philippi after the Lord had given Paul a vision of a man from Macedonia (the province in which Philippi was located). In this vision, the man pleaded with Paul to help those who were living there. Under the guidance of this vision, Paul and Silas charted new territory as they left Asia Minor, where they had done their work up to that point, and sailed for what was once the home of Alexander the Great.

In Philippi, Paul and Silas encountered new blessings and challenges. Without a Jewish synagogue for a home base, they resorted to starting their work at what they assumed would be a place of prayer by a river. God blessed their efforts and gave them the opportunity to share the gospel with an affluent woman named Lydia, who was in the lucrative business of selling the purple dye used in fine cloth. At the same time, however, Satan was at work among these people bereft of the good news of Jesus, and one of the visible demonstrations of that fact was that he had sent one of his demons to possess a young servant girl. This delighted her masters because this demon allowed her to prognosticate the future and afforded them a chance for profit. After some time witnessing this spectacle, Paul could endure it no longer. In Jesus' name, he drove out the demon and released this girl from Satan's clutches. This act of mercy invoked rage from the girl's owners because they would no longer rake in the profits from her demonic predictions. They had Paul and Silas beaten and thrown into prison where they no doubt suffered as stocks bound their feet. God, however, had not abandoned his servants. He sent an earthquake and broke them free from their captivity. In the process, he also blessed them with the opportunity to witness to the prison keeper who was ready to take his own life at the prospect of losing all his prisoners. The next day, the officials of the city released Paul and Silas and directed them to leave their jurisdiction. It may have appeared an unlikely way to build a church in Philippi, but through it all, God was at work. Lydia, the prison keeper, and others joined Paul in confessing Christ as their Savior and called on his name for the forgiveness of their sins. Where it seemed most unlikely to human reason, God created faith through the working of his Word and sacraments.

That faith didn't stop with confessing the truth with the mouth. It leaped into action. When Paul wrote back to the new congregation of believers in Philippi, he praised them. Among all the congregations Paul had founded and served, they stood out in their ongoing support for Paul and his gospel ministry. "Moreover, as you Philippians know," Paul wrote, "in the early days of your acquaintance with the gospel, when I set out from Macedonia, not one church shared with me in the matter of giving and receiving, except you only; for even when I was in Thessalonica, you sent me aid more than once when I was in need" (Philippians 4:15,16). The Philippians, who did not know the gospel of Jesus long before this and needed believers entrusted with the secret things of God to make the gospel known to them, now had great concern both for the one who brought them that good news and for those Paul would continue to serve. Their faith in Jesus produced a new life, a life of good works.

The vine and the branches

The Philippians were living examples of a truth Jesus taught his disciples about faith. As the Lord walked with them to the Garden of Gethsemane on the night before his death, he used a picture that would have been familiar to them. "I am the vine; you are the branches. If you remain in me and I in you, you will bear much fruit; apart from me you can do nothing" (John 15:5). Like a vine, Jesus is the source of life. A vine brings water and nutrients to all the branches that come from it. Likewise, Jesus brings God's forgiveness, grace, and blessing to all who are connected to him through faith. That's why Jesus can speak about himself with exclusive terms. He is the only way, the only truth, the only life (John 14:6). His is the only name under heaven by which we must and will be saved (Acts 4:12). Yes, it is only the connection a person has to Christ through faith that can save. That is why we confess that we are saved by faith. It is not the faith itself that merits our salvation; rather, faith is the means, or the tool, that God uses to connect us to Christ, the one who earned our salvation by his perfect life and innocent death.

That connection to Christ also has a great effect on our lives on this earth. A vine's connection to the branch transfers life to the branch, and not only life but the fruits of life as well. The branch lives because it receives everything it needs for life from the vine, but it also means that the branch is going to produce something: fruit. A gardener would be foolish if he looked for fruit on branches that had fallen off from the vine. Such a gardener would be a laughingstock to anyone who saw him. On the other hand, a farmer inspecting branches connected to the vine for the fruit of the harvest would be doing exactly what everyone would expect. Branches connected to the vine naturally produce fruit. It's what they do.

The parallel for Christians concerns our lives of good works. The gift of faith the Holy Spirit has implanted within our hearts is not mere intellectual knowledge. Faith doesn't mean simply having the right information in our heads without that information having any effect on our lives. The gift of faith is a living thing. It gives rise to a Christian life, and that Christian life shows itself with good works. Our faith produces fruit, to carry on with Jesus' metaphor of the vine and branches. Just as a branch connected to a vine produces fruit, so a Christian connected to Christ through faith produces good works.

Faith produces fruit, not the other way around. Sometimes human nature wants to reverse the relationship and operate as though it is the fruits that produce the faith, as though the fruits are responsible for saving us. Such a view, however, is really no different than imagining that apples hanging from a tree's branches make an apple tree. This view confuses the relationship. The tree has not grown from the apples on its branches, but the apples have grown from the tree. Likewise, faith produces good works. They flow from a heart of faith. Good works, however, cannot produce a believer. In fact, without faith, good works are impossible from the beginning. It would be like expecting an evergreen tree to produce apples.

The necessity of fruits

At the same time, we dare not use the relationship of faith and works to minimize the importance of those works. Sinful human nature tries to downplay fruits of faith and, in doing so, reduce faith to an inert thing. The apostle James met such lies head-on. To those who wanted to insist that the content of their lives didn't matter as long as they had the right knowledge, James issued a strong warning: "What good is it, my brothers and sisters, if someone claims to have faith but has no deeds? Can such faith save them? Suppose a brother or a sister is without clothes and daily food. If one of you says to them, 'Go in peace; keep warm and well fed,' but does nothing about their physical needs, what good is it? In the same way, faith by itself, if it is not accompanied by action, is dead" (James 2:14-

17). Someone who claims to have faith but refuses to produce fruits of faith is no different than a branch cut off from the vine, a dead unbeliever.

These words from James serve as an important alarm, especially to those who have enjoyed the blessing of the knowledge of Jesus for many years. How easy it is to say to oneself, "I am a member of a church. I went to catechism class when I was young. I know Jesus as my Savior. I know the right things, but I don't want to trouble myself with following God's Word. After all, Jesus will forgive me. What difference does it make if anyone knows about my faith? What difference does it make if I have any fruits of faith at all?" To such sinful arrogance, James' words issue a call to turn away from such foolishness. A faith like that is dead. In other words, it is a sham faith, really no faith at all.

But what about the conscientious believer who examines his or her life and says, "Woe is me! I have no fruits to show for my faith. I am just an ordinary person without much to show for my years of Christian living. I go to church. I go to work. I take the kids to school, but fruits of faith? I can't think of the last time I had time to volunteer at church for something extra. I don't think I'm very good at telling other people about my faith. Does that mean that I am cut off from the vine? Does that mean my faith is the dead faith James is talking about?"

Fears like that parallel the words of the believers in Jesus' description of the end of the world and the final judgment. Jesus had appeared and welcomed his people to come to him and enjoy the eternal inheritance of God's kingdom prepared for them. As evidence of their faith, he pointed to the fruit their faith had produced in their lives. "I was hungry and you gave me something to eat, I was thirsty and you gave me something to drink, I was a stranger and you invited me in, I needed clothes and you clothed me, I was sick and you looked after me, I was in prison and you came to visit me" (Matthew 25:35,36). These believers had done some wonderful works for their Savior as their faith expressed itself through love and produced a life full of fruit.

The believers themselves, however, weren't so sure. They took a look at their lives and did not see the magnificent fruits Jesus had pointed out. Could Jesus have made a mistake? Of course not! But, nevertheless, they inquired of the Lord, "Lord, when did we do all these things?" Jesus encouraged them one more time and said, "Truly I tell you, whatever you did for one of the least of these brothers and sisters of mine, you did for me" (Matthew 25:40).

All believers can take comfort in that encouragement Jesus will offer his people at the end of the world. Living the Christian life doesn't mean taking a daily tally of the fruits our faith produces, no more than an apple tree keeps an inventory of the apples it produces. The fruits come naturally. In the same way, Christians produce fruit as a natural result of faith. That means not every fruit of faith will be a deliberate act; we won't necessarily be conscious of every good work as we carry it out.

In fact, living the Christian life doesn't mean we need to spend time worrying about producing fruits of faith in sufficient quantity or quality. Rather, just as faith is God's working within us and is his gift to us, so the fruits our faith produces are really his works too. Paul offered that encouragement to the Ephesians.

In his description of believers he says, "We are God's handiwork, created in Christ Jesus to do good works, which God prepared in advance for us to do" (Ephesians 2:10). Isn't that a remarkable encouragement? First, God fashioned and made us as his own handiwork. He did that through our Savior Jesus. He cleansed us from our sin in the blood of his own Son. He clothed us with that Son's righteousness and gave us a new life. In Christ, we are a new creation, a product of God's workmanship. Now, what is the result of God's work? We are not just an arts-and-craft project that sits on a shelf somewhere to collect dust. No, God's workmanship produces even more. It is living and active. It produces fruits of faith. Still, there's an additional evidence of God's grace in that passage. The good works we carry out—our fruits of faith—aren't random acts we come across in life, nor are they things we come up with on our own. Instead, they are works God has prepared ahead of time for us to do. Think of it! In God's good and gracious governance of all creation, in his perfect foreknowledge of all things, he has prepared ways for our faith to reflect itself through good works. He puts them in our path as a gift of his grace. We have no need then, to fret, and worry that somehow we haven't produced enough fruits of faith and therefore have forfeited the blessings of faith that are ours in Christ Jesus. When those fears assail us, we can cling ever closer to our Savior and rest easy in the same promise he gave to those on his right in his description of the Last Day: "Truly I tell you, whatever you did for one of the least of these brothers and sisters of mine, you did for me."

Likewise, we may sometimes worry that so many of our deeds are not worthy of the title "fruits of faith." We observe other people doing great and commendable works such as volunteering in foreign countries or donating huge sums of money to charitable causes. We might think that we have never done anything of such grandeur, and that our works pale in comparison to such offerings.

Jesus' Word comforts us in those concerns as well. "Whatever you did . . . you did for me," he tells us. Why do parents love their children's gifts? Isn't it because they love their children? Isn't it true that parents would love a gift their child offers, given in love, even if the gift itself isn't that desirable? Of course they would, because it's not the gift but the fact that a dear child is giving it to them. When we think about it, we realize it's really not so much about the intrinsic value of the gifts themselves at all. Often, young children can't afford, nor do they have the skill, to offer their parents a gift that is worthy in and of itself. Parents, nevertheless, delight to receive gifts from their children. They prize that work of art made in a school classroom as though it deserves a place at a great museum. They put it in a prized place on the refrigerator or on their office wall or desktop so they can see it often. What matters to them is that their little child made it for them, and for that reason, it has great value to them.

In his grace, Jesus receives our fruits in the same way. He values them not because they have such great value in themselves but because of who we are. We are his blood-bought people, his dear children. Through faith, we are children of God through faith in Christ Jesus (Galatians 3:27). When our heavenly Father sees our works, therefore, he sees works of his precious children. He delights in them because we did them for him.

That truth adds wonderful meaning to our day-to-day lives. We need not seek out some extraordinary life in order to produce fruits of faith and serve the Lord. The Lord takes care of that for us. He prepares the fruit in advance for us to do. He delights to view our day-to-day works and lives as good works that are pleasing to him. When a Christian mother and father care for their children, when a Christian employee carries out her work with faithfulness and without complaint, when a Christian student completes the assignments his teacher asks of him—all of these are wonderful works offered to our gracious God.

To the world, such works pass by unnoticed. To the world, nothing is special about any of those acts. To the Lord, however, such works are precious because his children do them. They do these works for him, and he delights in them.

The necessity of faith

God delights in his children serving him, and we are his children through faith. Works that are pleasing to the Lord, therefore, must come from faith. As a result, many of the works this world lauds as the greatest works of humankind do not please the Lord at all. An unbeliever, for example, can make great breakthroughs in science that produce wonderful results for the world. An unbeliever can make generous, yes outstanding, efforts in philanthropy and in so doing improve the lives of many in this world. To human society, these works outshine the works of many, if not most, Christians. What, however, is the Lord's verdict? Toward the end of his book, the prophet Isaiah offers a stunning appraisal of humanity's acts of righteousness. Acts that human beings regard to be righteous but are not done in faith the Lord regards to be filthy rags (Isaiah 64:6). To human reason, this appears as nothing but madness. "It's not right! It's unfair!" human nature protests. How can God give such a condemning evaluation of what seems to be so good to the world?

The answer is faith. "Apart from me," Jesus tells us, "you can do nothing" (John 15:5). Apart from faith in Jesus, we are not God's children but children of the devil. Apart from the relationship we have with our loving Father through faith in Christ Jesus, we remain in rebellion against God and his enemies. Our works, therefore, no matter how impressive to the world, cannot please him.

To humankind, this standard makes no sense, but the Lord's thoughts are not ours (Isaiah 55:9). He is almighty. Nothing is beyond his grasp. He is the Creator of all things. "The earth is the LORD's, and everything in it" (Psalm 24:1). He really doesn't need any work of humankind, no matter how impressive it might seem to us. He doesn't rely on our efforts to accomplish anything.

How would a second-grade art project compare to the work of Leonardo da Vinci? Perhaps one second grader has more artistic gifts than another. Perhaps one second grader is the best second-grade artist in all the world and receives accolades for such visible talent at a young age. Still, in comparison to da Vinci, a second grader is just not going to measure up, no matter how good she is in comparison to her peers.

In the same way, no human work—no matter how great that work appears to our human nature—can impress the living God on its own merits. It is too small, too insignificant—just like the artistic offerings of a second grader. What, therefore, is the difference between a work that delights the Lord and a work that remains meaningless? The difference lies in the one who is doing the work. For the unbeliever who remains God's enemy, any work is unacceptable and worthless in his sight. For a believer, a fruit of faith is precious in God's sight.

As you think about your own faith, consider the ways the Lord has prepared for you to reflect that faith through good works, like he did for those Philippian believers. Give thanks to God for giving you that grace. Ask him to provide even more of those opportunities. If you have begun to think that showing your faith isn't that important, take to heart Jesus' warning that his Father will cut off every branch that fails to bear fruit. At the same time, if you are afraid that your fruits don't measure up, then find your faith's assurance in your Savior, who not only forgives you for your shortcomings but also lifts you up as he calls you his own. Remember, he is the one who gives you the ability and the opportunity to serve him. In him, you have nothing to fear. ♥

5

I Know That
My Faith Needs Nourishing

Jesus describes himself as a shepherd, the Good Shepherd in fact. Though few people in an industrialized world live and work as animal caretakers, the image of the Good Shepherd still brings comfort.

Sheep need someone to care for them. By themselves, their place on the food chain means they stand little chance of surviving. By themselves, the wolves and other wild foes would attack and destroy them. The sheep need a shepherd.

And it's not just predators that necessitate the shepherd. Sheep need someone to look out for their daily needs as well, for their food and drink. The shepherd, therefore, leads the sheep to pastures full of the green grass upon which the sheep can graze. He takes them to quiet waters—not the rushing waters of the rapids that could sweep them away and drown them—but the gently flowing streams from which they can take their drink. A shepherd sees to the sheep's everyday needs.

No one fails to see the necessity in that. Without the shepherd to feed the sheep, the sheep in no time would starve or die of thirst. Without the shepherd to watch over them, the sheep would face almost certain death at the mercy of their foes. Without the shepherd and what the shepherd gives them, the sheep would be in a wretched condition indeed.

A sheep does not just depend on the shepherd some of the time or only at certain stages of life. No, because the shepherd provides for the daily protection and needs of the sheep, it follows that the shepherd needs to be a part of the sheep's life on a regular, ongoing, daily basis.

What an accurate picture of our relationship with our Savior Jesus the description of a shepherd provides. Without him, we would be in just such a wretched condition, only not simply in a physical sense but, far more importantly, in a spiritual one.

What is true of the sheep's earthly need for a shepherd is true of our need for a spiritual shepherd. We cannot decide that we only need our spiritual Shepherd where and when it suits us, perhaps once or twice a year. Nor can we think that the Shepherd can tend to us while we are young, perhaps while in grade school and then perhaps again once we've settled down or are getting along in years. No, we need our Shepherd throughout our lives. We need his care on an ongoing basis.

We need our Good Shepherd because of the nature of faith. God's gift of faith is not some kind of artifact that we can place on our shelves to admire when we happen to notice it yet comfortably leave without a second thought if we are going away for an extended period of time or if we just aren't interested in it for a while.

Faith is a living thing. We might compare it to a delicate houseplant or a pet. Because it is living, it needs our continual care and attention. If we have a pet, then we need to feed and water it. We need to give it time to exercise and play. Especially if it's still young and maturing, we need to give it the personal attention it so craves. Otherwise it will cry and complain. It will languish. In the worst of circumstances of abuse and neglect, it could even die.

The same is true of a plant. Depending on the species, it may require more or less deliberate care, but it still has needs. It needs sunlight, water, and the right kind of soil. Without these things, it may hang on to life for a while, maybe even a long time, but in the end it depends on those things for life. Without somcone altending to its needs, it cannot survive.

Our faith is a living thing. Just as parents might give their young child a pet with the instructions, "Now, taking care of him is your responsibility," so God has given us the responsibility of caring for the faith he has given us.

Guarding the gift

When Paul wrote to young pastor Timothy, he gave this instruction: "Timothy, guard what has been entrusted to your care" (1 Timothy 6:20). To Paul, this was not something to approach with a casual attitude. To guard something implies that someone thinks highly of something. It is valuable, precious. To guard something implies that a person is taking deliberate action to ensure something's security. One might think of all the effort people exert to guard things that are precious in this life. Devices like safes, security systems, and cameras, and even trained and armed guards are enlisted for protecting valuable people and things. That is the attitude Paul wanted Timothy (and us) to have toward our faith.

Faith, however, is not something that we can keep safe with a physical lock and key or even a state-of-the-art security system. As a spiritual gift, guarding faith means something different than guarding our physical body or possessions. It means we keep it from that which threatens to hurt or harm it. It also means we make a diligent effort to keep that faith strong so that it withstands the attacks that will still inevitably come in this life. Therefore we will want to tend to it and nurture it as the living thing that it is.

Faith doesn't need physical food and water, of course, nor does it need sunlight like a plant does. There's really only one thing that keeps faith strong, and it's the same thing that the Holy Spirit uses to create faith in the first place: the gospel.

The gospel creates faith. In addition, the gospel nourishes and keeps our faith strong. The first verses of the book of Psalms describe this relationship most beautifully:

Blessed is the one
who does not walk in step with the wicked
or stand in the way that sinners take
or sit in the company of mockers,
but whose delight is in the law of the LORD,
and who meditates on his law day and night.
That person is like a tree planted by streams of water,
which yields its fruit in season
and whose leaf does not wither—
whatever they do prospers. (1:1-3)

In the Great Plains of the United States, one can observe a situation similar to the one David describes. Much of the landscape, especially in the heat of the summer months, is too dry to support any vegetation beyond grasses. So, unlike some wetter areas of the country, the Great Plains have few naturally occurring trees or forests. Instead, sprawling grasslands extend for mile after mile. Interrupting these seamless oceans of grassland, however, flows the occasional river or stream. If the river holds enough water, then a row of trees will sprout that traces the river's path through the otherwise open fields. The streams of water give life to trees that would otherwise have no hope of survival.

Like that tree planted by the river, so is the person of faith in this world. In a desert of spiritual death, the believer has sprung to new life by faith, the Holy Spirit's gracious gift. And the Holy Spirit does not forsake those he has blessed with faith. Instead, he dwells within them; he makes their bodies his temple (1 Corinthians 6:19). And as he dwells with us, he continues to keep and strengthen us in his gift of faith. He does that through his chosen means, the gospel in Word and sacrament (Romans 10:17).

The need for the Word

It's no coincidence that Psalm 1 connects a life rich in the Lord's Word with an image of a thriving life. The two go hand in hand. Through the good news of Jesus the Holy Spirit creates faith. It is through that same Word the Holy Spirit keeps us in faith, and through that faith we have spiritual life.

It's why God so often describes his Word as a life-giving thing. He said through his Old Testament prophet Isaiah, "As the rain and the snow come down from heaven, and do not return to it without watering the earth and making it bud and flourish, so that it yields seed for the sower and bread for the eater, so is my word that goes out from my mouth: It will not return to me empty, but will accomplish what I desire and achieve the purpose for which I sent it" (55:10,11). Likewise, Jesus himself says in the gospel of John, "The Spirit gives life; the flesh counts for nothing. The words I have spoken to you—they are full of the Spirit and life" (John 6:63). God's Word gives life.

Just as we do not question eating and drinking everyday (for most of us, we could hardly imagine not doing so), so it is good for us to recognize our regular need for the life-giving nourishment that God's Word provides our faith. We need it. We need it so much that we must be on guard. We must guard against anything that would crowd it out of our lives or attitudes that would lead us to act as though it weren't that important, or daily habits that leave little time for that Word which matters above all else.

God warns us about the potential consequences of such neglect of God's Word. One of the congregations John addressed at the beginning of Revelation was in that danger.

"To the angel of the church in Laodicea write:

These are the words of the Amen, the faithful and true witness, the ruler of God's creation. I know your deeds, that you are neither cold nor hot. I wish you were either one or the other! So, because you are lukewarm—neither hot nor cold—I am about to spit you out of my mouth. You say, 'I am rich; I have acquired wealth and do not need a thing.' But you do not realize that you are wretched, pitiful, poor, blind and naked. I counsel you to buy from me gold refined in the fire, so you can become rich; and white clothes to wear, so you can cover your shameful nakedness; and salve to put on your eyes, so you can see.

Those whom I love I rebuke and discipline. So be earnest and repent. Here I am! I stand at the door and knock. If anyone hears my voice and opens the door, I will come in and eat with that person, and they with me.

To the one who is victorious, I will give the right to sit with me on my throne, just as I was victorious and sat down with my Father on his throne. Whoever has ears, let them hear what the Spirit says to the churches." (3:14-22)

If Christians relegate faith to an unimportant place in their lives, the results can be disastrous. Without the nourishment and strengthening of God's Word and Sacrament, that faith will grow colder and colder. Eventually, it will die altogether.

Apparently that mind-set was threatening the church in Laodicea. Their attitude was telling. They had the attitude that their faith was secure. They thought they were "rich" in Jesus' words. They imagined they had no need for the strength and nourishment God provides through his means of grace.

Their attitude, in itself, is a teachable moment for us. When we believe our faith to be secure is when we find ourselves in danger. No doubt it's why the apostle Paul offered a parallel warning in his letter to the Corinthians: "If you think you are standing firm, be careful that you don't fall!" (1 Corinthians 10:12). Standing firm isn't the problem. In fact, it is a frequent encouragement of Paul to the congregations he served to "stand firm" (1 Corinthians 16:13; Philippians 1:27; 2 Thessalonians 2:15). No, it was the thinking, or dare we say, the imagining that there really is no need for any concern because we are already standing firm by our own strength and ability outside of God's strengthening through his gospel.

When we allow ourselves to fall into that kind of spiritual apathy and indifference, we deprive our faith of the nourishment it so desperately needs. That's why Jesus pleaded with his words to the Laodiceans to recognize their need. They were still his beloved people. They hadn't lost faith completely. He wanted nothing more than for them to wake up and return to him to strengthen what they had.

When it comes to the Laodiceans, we don't have the rest of the story, so to speak. We don't know if they took these words of warning to heart and applied them to their lives. Perhaps one day in heaven we will know.

What we can do, however, is apply these words to our own lives. Especially for the many Christians of our age who enjoy unsurpassed opportunities to hear and study God's Word, the temptation to think of these things as trifles that will always be available should we want them is just as prevalent as it was among the Laodiceans, perhaps even more so.

This temptation strikes often among young adults who have known the Christian faith from childhood. Perhaps they grew up in a Christian home. They had Christian parents who brought them to church and Sunday school. Maybe they even attended a Christian school so that God's Word was a part of their daily lives. Catechism classes and confirmation may have been rites of passage for such young people.

But then they grow up, and perhaps all of that Christianity stuff can start seeming a bit childish to them. Maybe they imagine they just don't have need of it any more. Or perhaps they still profess a faith in the Savior, but they just don't think they need to hear God's Word so often anymore since they already know enough about it anyway.

Yes, if someone is certain that their faith is indestructible, that because they were once saved they will always be saved, then that person is in grave spiritual danger. The devil delights in welcoming such ones to share in his eternal destruction.

It is to these people, as well as others who may be in different circumstances in life but have fallen into the same general mind-set, that God's Word speaks in the strongest possible terms. "Wake up! You are wretched, poor, pitiful, blind! Return to me so that you can reclaim the treasure that is yours through faith in Christ!"

The antidote is always the same. It is not our human effort or willpower. It is not our telling ourselves that we can remain strong on our own. No, it is the tree planted by streams of living water that thrives. It is the one who goes to the Good Shepherd who finds care and protection and strength to face each day. That's why each one of us needs God's Word for our faith always and often.

Perhaps the devil can tempt us from time to time into thinking that regularly attending worship and Bible study to hear God's Word isn't making any difference in our lives. "I've heard it all before. I don't feel like it's doing anything for my faith anyways. I sing the same old songs over and over again. The sermons all sound the same to me. I can't remember much about them after a few weeks pass by anyways. What difference does it really make?"

Most Christians have probably felt that way at one time or another. Remember, the devil will do anything to get us away from Jesus' words. So how do we combat this attitude in our lives?

In a similar way, consider how none of us could even come close to remembering each meal we have eaten. We might recall one particularly sumptuous meal at a fine restaurant. Maybe we relish our favorites that Grandma used to make us. But remember *everything* we've ever eaten? There's no chance of it. Likewise, many other meals we've eaten probably don't deserve to be remembered anyways. Maybe they came from a box or a can from the grocery store and were relatively unremarkable as far as meals go. The thing is, even those meals nourished our bodies and gave us strength for the tasks of the day.

Do you see how the same is true for our spiritual nourishment? Some of our spiritual meals are memorable. Maybe it's a Christmas or an Easter service that was lovely and uplifting from beginning to end. Maybe it was a sermon that touched your soul with just what you needed to hear in a particular moment of your life. Those things are blessed moments indeed, and most times, they're also unpredictable and unplanned.

At the same time, other services might seem less uplifting and encouraging. They might seem routine or even dry. Maybe the hymns were difficult to sing. The pastor seemed lost in the sermon. It was more like one of those meals from a box. But even in those moments, don't discount the fact that the Holy Spirit is still nourishing you through God's Word. He's still giving you the strength you need to face each day. Maybe you won't remember anything in particular from a service like that after a few weeks, but because the Holy Spirit works through his Word, it was still good for your faith.

Caring for our faith is important, so we are wise to give careful thought to it, even to have a thought-out plan to care for it. Regular public worship, for example, where pastors (under-shepherds of the Good Shepherd) feed us with instruction from God's Word and where we confess our faith with fellow believers is something that every Christian will want to make use of as much as possible. Personal time in God's Word with devotions is not just something to do once in a while but can be a regular habit that brings great profit and direction to life. The Bible studies that many Christian congregations offer are not something only for the really religious, but they can be something that all can use and benefit from.

The opportunities for learning and instruction have never been more abundant. They are the things God uses to strengthen and keep us in our faith, the most precious possession we have. May we learn to treasure it as such all the days of our lives and to put that attitude into practice in our lives, so that in ordering our lives we give ample opportunities for God to nourish us with his life-giving Word. ❤

6

I Know That
My Faith Needs Refining

The man had great faith, one of the greatest examples of faith in all history. His faith, in fact, has earned him the name "the father of those who believe." That man's name was Abram.

Abram had many opportunities to put his faith into practice. He lived in Harran, a city in Mesopotamia, but God instructed him to pick up everything he owned, leave his homeland, and travel to Canaan. God promised Abram that his descendants would one day own that land, but to date, Abram didn't have any landholdings in this foreign country. Speaking of descendants, Abram and his wife Sarai didn't have any children either. Best of all his promises, God revealed to Abram that through him God would bless all the nations of the earth. The New Testament makes explicit what was already evident in the Old Testament: Through Abram, God would send the long-awaited Anointed One, the offspring of Eve who would crush the devil's head and destroy his work (Genesis 3:15). Again, however, how exactly God would fulfill that most gracious promise when Abram didn't even have a single child was unclear to say the least.

But God came through, as believers know he always does. At long last, when Abram (whom God renamed Abraham, which means "father of many") was 100 years old and his wife Sarai (whom God renamed Sarah) was 90 years old and well past her natural time for bearing children, God blessed the two of them with the gift of a son, little Isaac. At long last, Abraham could give thanks for this special gift of God, and not only that, but he could begin to see the avenue by which God was going to bring all his promises to fulfillment. Through Isaac, God would make Abraham into a great nation that would inherit the Promised Land flowing with milk and honey. Abraham's faith in God's promise at last had visible and tangible fulfillment in his son Isaac. That faith Abraham had guarded with a steadfast spirit could at last rest in some visible, tangible proof of what God had promised.

But then came God's command, and it was unthinkable. "Take your son, your only son, whom you love—Isaac—and go to the region of Moriah. Sacrifice him there as a burnt offering on a mountain I will show you" (Genesis 22:2).

It doesn't require the experience of being a parent to understand the gut punch these words must have been to Abraham, but for those who have been parents, these words strike the soul with an even sharper pain.

How could God? Why would God command Abraham to do such a thing? For many it appears to be unthinkable cruelty. Here was this only son born to Abraham and Sarah in their old age, this delight of their hearts, who, in addition to the joy that all children bring to their parents, was the personification of God's promises, and yet now, God himself was commanding Abraham to throw it all away. Isn't human reason naturally appalled, yes even angry at God's command to Abraham?

From Abraham, however, we hear no objection or protest against the Lord's word. Instead, Genesis relates that "early the next morning" (22:3), Abraham got up to carry out the Lord's instructions. He took Isaac and two servants, along with the necessary articles for the sacrifice, and departed for the place the Lord had told him about.

One can hardly imagine the anguish of the journey. To make it all the worse, Isaac spoke up with a question as they walked along: "Father? . . . The fire and wood are here, . . . but where is the lamb for the burnt offering?" (Genesis 22:7). How could a loving father even bear to answer a question like that?

In spite of the unimaginable difficulty of it all, Abraham remained faithful to the word of the Lord. He built an altar, arranged the wood, and tied up his son. With the strength of his faith, Abraham was determined to carry out God's command, even up to the point that he took the sacrificial blade in his hands with the intent of plunging it into his own son.

The angel of the LORD called out to him from heaven, "Abraham! Abraham!"

"Here I am," Abraham replied.

"Do not lay a hand on the boy," he said. "Do not do anything to him. Now I know that you fear God, because you have not withheld from me your son, your only son." (Genesis 22:11,12)

The whole ordeal had been a test. God had never intended for Abraham to kill Isaac. Instead, God presented this man of great faith with a situation to put his faith in the Lord's word into practice, a situation where almost anybody else would have walked away from God once and for all. Abraham, on the other hand, acted in faith where so few could have succeeded. He was willing to give up his own son to remain faithful to the Lord. Though the Lord stayed his faithful servant's hand, in his heart Abraham had indeed sacrificed Isaac (Hebrews 11:17).

Was it a cruel joke? Divine amusement? Why would God put Abraham through such an ordeal, such mental and spiritual anguish?

We don't always know why God acts in the way he does. The life of Job, an Old Testament believer, proves that. Job did not understand why such horrible afflictions invaded his thus-far blessed life. His friends presumed that Job must have sinned against the Lord in some way and brought divine retribution on himself. Those friends, however, were wrong. Through the insight of inspired Scripture we learn what Job did not know. His sufferings were an opportunity for him to glorify God in the face of the devil's assertion that if Job suffered he would give up his faith. As a result, Job had to endure losing his property and wealth, his health, and even his own children without any knowledge of what was going on behind the scenes. He didn't know why God permitted such trouble in his life. The same is often true in the lives of believers today.

With spiritual maturity, we can recognize this truth not as a frustration but as a comfort. If we could wrap our mind around every one of the almighty God's thoughts, he wouldn't be any bigger or smarter than we are. In reality, he is infinitely bigger and smarter than all of us put together, so much so the church father Augustine famously observed that for us to comprehend God would be like trying to put all the ocean's waters in a small hole in the sand of the beach. Yes, God tells us, "As the heavens are higher than the earth, so are my ways higher than your ways and my thoughts than your thoughts" (Isaiah 55:9).

The necessity of tests

So why does God allow our faith to endure such difficult tests? Though we cannot hope to comprehend everything God does or the reasons for which he does it, he has told us something about the tests of faith he sometimes chooses to put his people through. Through James, he tells us, "Consider it pure joy, my brothers and sisters, whenever you face trials of many kinds, because you know that the testing of your faith produces perseverance. Let perseverance finish its work so that you may be mature and complete, not lacking anything" (1:2-4). Likewise, through the apostle Peter the Lord tells us, "Now for a little while you may have had to suffer grief in all kinds of trials. These have come so that the proven genuineness of your faith— of greater worth than gold, which perishes even though refined by fire—may result in praise, glory and honor when Jesus Christ is revealed" (1 Peter 1:6,7). Yes, God tells us that he uses tests of faith for the good of our faith.

Let's return to the example of Abraham. God had no need to find out what Abraham would do when he instructed him to sacrifice his son. God knows all things, and before him nothing is hidden. "In their hearts humans plan their course, but the LORD establishes their steps" (Proverbs 16:9). Nothing in all creation—past, present, or future—is hidden from his all-knowing sight. God, therefore, had nothing to find out by putting Abraham through this test of faith.

Instead, God who works all things for the good of those who love him (Romans 8:28) used a test of faith for Abraham's good. Even though the hours of that test brought Abraham heart-rending difficulty, consider how it served to strengthen his already remarkable faith. For one, it demonstrated to him that he could rely on God and his Word even in the most uncertain circumstances. Yes, God would make sure that his promises remained intact. For another, it showed to Abraham that God had blessed him with such a faith that he could endure even this most difficult test. As he looked back on it, Abraham could reflect on the evidence of that test and know that God had given him a faith that could withstand the greatest trials and tribulations. Perhaps Abraham could even compare this test with past occasions in his life (like when he was deceptive about Sarah being his wife because of his fear of what might happen to him) and could see for himself how much he had grown in faith over the years. Yes, Abraham could see that he indeed feared, loved, and trusted in his God, of course not perfectly because he remained a sinner like all people, but as a child of God whom God had blessed with great faith.

That great faith also tells us why God prepared such a difficult test for Abraham. Consider that God had already blessed Abraham with an outstanding faith, a model for believers of all time to emulate. What kind of test, then, would serve to strengthen a faith like Abraham's?

Imagine an Olympic weight lifter wanted to improve his performance. What kind of workout would he need to complete to bring about that goal? No doubt, the workout would involve some strenuous tasks, something no ordinary person could handle. If the Olympian did the same workout that the average person at the local gym did several times a week, would that help him achieve his goal? We could assume such a workout would be easy for the world-class weight lifter to complete in a shorter time, but we can also see that it wouldn't really do much good. It wouldn't push him to advance to the level necessary to compete at the Olympic level. No, the Olympian needs an Olympic-level workout, something so difficult and strenuous that the average gym-goer probably couldn't complete it at all.

In the same way, consider how Abraham's faith needed an Olympic-level test. If he was going to grow in his faith, if this test was going to push him to new heights, it needed to be the kind of test that the average believer would very likely have failed. A great faith requires a great test.

So how does God use tests to grow our faith? It bears repeating that we do not and cannot understand everything about how and why God chooses to use tests of faith in our lives. Some believers seem to experience a more test-laden life. Others (at least from an external perspective) seem to dance through life with far fewer difficulties. Sometimes when a time of testing comes into a believer's life, it seems like those tests never stop, as one test follows closely on the footsteps of another. Other times, we may experience a lull in tests to our faith. Again, we can't know God's plan for all these things. His understanding far surpasses our own. That's why a general principle to keep in mind while pondering this question (and many others) is that we can be certain about God's will only when he reveals it to us in his Word.

In spite of our limitations, however, we can still observe the general rule that God uses testing for the good of faith, both in ourselves and in others. Bear in mind how God's testing of our faith is worlds apart from the purposes of the devil in the temptations he puts in our path. The devil puts temptations in our path as obstacles to trip us up. His goal is to pull us away from our Savior. Like he wanted Job to do, he wants us and all believers to forsake the Lord. God, on the other hand, never tests us with that intent. His goal is just the opposite: to produce a blessing for our faith. James, the biblical author who explained the blessing of trials, just a few verses later clarifies as he writes, "When tempted, no one should say, 'God is tempting me.' For God cannot be tempted by evil, nor does he tempt anyone" (1:13). Yes, God only tests our faith for our good, never to hurt or harm us.

However, just as it was true for Abraham and Job, that doesn't mean those trials are easy or pleasant. God may use a devastating illness, for example, to teach us to call on him in our time of trouble. That illness may serve to refocus our earthly life on the eternal life that awaits us in heaven. It may even give us the opportunity to testify about our faith to others, especially when they see how we handle a devastating illness so much differently than an unbeliever does who does not have hope in God's promises. Yes, even something as unpleasant as an earthly sickness God could use for our spiritual good. Likewise, an economic hardship might teach us to look to him for daily bread, or a fractured relationship may draw us closer in our relationship to him.

At times, God could even use our tests of faith for the good of others. Imagine someone who has experienced a time of testing. God has used that testing to strengthen that person's faith. Isn't it a wonderful blessing when God can use that believer down the road to strengthen another believer who is now experiencing something similar?

Far from it! We can praise and thank God for the good times he gives us. We can pray that he keeps times of testing rare. Even if, by God's grace, we aren't experiencing a test of faith at a given time, there is still value in the growth of our faith. In other words, even if we don't see God testing our faith in particular ways, it can be valuable for us to consider how we can keep testing that faith ourselves.

Self-examination

The apostle Paul puts it this way to the Corinthians: "Examine yourselves to see whether you are in the faith; test yourselves. Do you not realize that Christ Jesus is in you—unless, of course, you fail the test?" (2 Corinthians 13:5).

How do students in a classroom prepare for a test? They might read a textbook or review their notes from class lectures, but a time comes when it's often helpful to test themselves. Maybe they cover up an answer in their notes and see if they know it without looking. Maybe they make flash cards and review key terms or concepts. The low stress of a personal test makes the actual test in class that much more manageable.

Sometimes it's easy to take our own faith for granted. (No doubt, that's sometimes why God himself will give us a test as a type of wake-up call, much like a teacher might give a pop quiz if she suspects her students have been lax in their work.) Taking our faith for granted, however, comes with far greater consequences. It's the difference between eternal life and eternal death. That's why God's Word gives stern warnings to believers who are backsliding in their faith. That's also why it's good for us to recognize these warnings and keep an eye on our faith as a regular habit.

Yes, our faith is precious, and it's not something we can tuck away into the back of our closets and forget about. If we do that, then we risk losing it altogether.

Testing our faith, therefore, as God tells us through Paul in 2 Corinthians is an important exercise for us. It is something that we want to consider on an individual basis.

How do we do that? A key point is to recognize *when* it's helpful to examine our faith. Just as a teacher gives the class a test because the students need the exercise of that test to keep them learning the material, so it is when we feel ourselves slipping in our faith that it can be helpful to test ourselves.

When we allow opportunities to hear God's Word and receive his Sacrament go by without our attendance, and when that begins to happen week in and week out, we can see the warning signs. When we start caring less that we follow God's Word in our lives, when his commandments begin to strike us as old-fashioned and suffocating rules that hamper our preferred style of living, then we can start to see that the devil is working his hardest to choke out our faith and destroy it. At such times, it's time to get our faith back in shape.

Examining our own faith can help us in that endeavor. Such an examination can focus on some very practical and measurable things. We can ask ourselves, "Have I been feeding and nourishing my faith through regular and frequent hearing of God's Word and receiving his Sacrament? Is my attendance at public worship with my fellow Christians increasing or decreasing? Do I make regular time during my daily life for reading God's Word on my own or for time in prayer, as God invites and commands me? Or have these habits slipped away in favor of other tasks and distractions? Am I living my faith on a day-to-day basis? Am I honoring the Lord with the time, talents, and treasures he has given me? Am I letting my light shine in this world so that others may see my good deeds and praise their Father in heaven, or would an observer of my life be hard-pressed to come up with any evidence that my life is any different from an unbeliever's?

When we examine our faith, we know that we will always find failures. We will always find room for improvement. That's because we are sinners one and all, and by nature we fall far short of the glory of God.

That's why together we rejoice in the sure and certain promise of forgiveness that God gives us. Through the merits and intercession of his dear Son Jesus, he has taken away our sin. We are his own precious, blood-bought children.

As God's forgiven children, we also want to keep growing. We want to grow closer to him day by day. We can welcome tests of faith into our lives, because we know our loving heavenly Father can and will use them for our spiritual good. That's why we can seek to examine our own faith, not as a point of pride or comparison to others, but as an opportunity to evaluate how we can grow ever closer to our Savior Jesus.

No test seems pleasant at the time. Certainly that was true for Abraham. Certainly that is true for us, and yet we can welcome such tests because they are good for our faith, a gift of God that is of greater worth than gold. ♥

7

I Know That
My Faith Struggles
With Doubts

It's a parent's worst nightmare. The father Jesus met was enduring the agony of watching his little boy suffer. A demon, one of the devil's minions, had set its sights on this man's child and had invaded his small frame. As if this physical possession were not enough, this demon had robbed this child of his ability to speak. It threw the boy to the ground, caused him to foam at the mouth like a rabid animal, and made him seize up as though dead. If nothing changed, his father feared his little boy really would be dead soon because, in addition to all the rest, that demon threw the boy's small frame into fire or water at every opportunity. The demon did it because it could. It didn't care whether the victim lived or died. Its interest was to inflict as much cruelty as it could. The father of this little boy wanted what any parent would; he wanted to find help for his young son. He would have given anything for it. Yes, he would have taken the suffering from that demon on himself if only it meant relief for his child.

The man's first attempt was met with failure. He went to Jesus' disciples and asked them to drive out the demon, but try as they might, their abilities fell short. The demon remained, while the disciples stood there helpless to intervene. Imagine the desperation the man must have felt in those moments. "No one can help my son! Not even the disciples of this famous rabbi can put an end to my son's torment!"

The man had one last chance. As he stood in the midst of a crowd before Jesus, the Teacher asked about all the commotion. The desperate man jumped at the opportunity to present his case to Jesus. He described his son's condition. He recounted the disciples' failure, and Jesus reacted: "'You unbelieving generation,' Jesus replied, 'how long shall I stay with you? How long shall I put up with you? Bring the boy to me'" (Mark 9:19). In the midst of the man's struggle, Jesus identified a perpetual problem among the people of Israel. Even as Jesus provided miracle after miracle, their hearts remained slow to believe. They wondered, "Can Jesus really do anything to help this time?"

As the boy appeared before Jesus, the demon continued its dirty work. It threw the boy's body to the ground and caused him to foam at the mouth. Jesus asked how long the boy had suffered in this way, and the man answered, "From childhood it has often thrown him into fire or water to kill him. But if you can do anything, take pity on us and help us" (Mark 9:21,22).

"If you can do anything..." In his answer, this father betrayed his feeling of hopelessness. "Maybe Jesus could do something, but I've already witnessed his disciples fail, so maybe Jesus will prove just as unable to help."

Jesus rebuked the man for his failure to believe. "'If you can'?" said Jesus. "Everything is possible for one who believes" (Mark 9:23). This man in his weakness and pain failed to believe a simple truth about God. All things are possible for him. "No word from God will ever fail" (Luke 1:37). What may be out of reach for any and every human being still bows before the will of the Almighty. Questioning the Lord's ability with the word *if* has no place in a believer's prayer. James makes this point in his letter when he writes, "If any of you lacks wisdom, you should ask God, who gives generously to all without finding fault, and it will be given to you. But when you ask, you must believe and not doubt, because the one who doubts is like a wave of the sea, blown and tossed by the wind. That person should not expect to receive anything from the Lord. Such a person is double-minded and unstable in all they do" (1:5-8).

That's a high standard James sets. When we approach God in prayer, we have no right to doubt. In fact, the Lord takes offense at our doubting when we ask him something because, in essence, we're doubting him. Imagine informing a teacher or boss of a minor problem at school or work. "I know you're really powerless to do anything about this problem, but I thought I would let you know anyhow." Maybe our evaluation of such an earthly situation could even be correct. Maybe a teacher or a boss really can't do anything to help us out of certain problems, but what about the Lord? What about when we present our prayers and petitions before his throne of grace? He tells us, and we know with certainty that he can help us in every need.

Tenacious doubt

Or do we? Does the exhortation from James sometimes cause us to blush with shame? Maybe we've known the true God and his Word for the greater part of our lives. We know his power. We know his promises. We know his love for us and, still, when when we find ourselves suffering with a situation like that man with a demon-possessed son, don't we find ourselves speaking the same language? "If you can do anything, Lord . . ." And maybe many of us would have to acknowledge that it doesn't take anything nearly as difficult as what that man was suffering to drive us to doubt our God. Even in the little things of life, we can fall into thinking and feeling like our prayers don't accomplish much of anything, like God is far distant from us and our problems, like his love and care for us are just abstract thoughts with no practical benefit for life in this world.

In moments of personal reflection, it can lead us to wonder, "Do I have faith at all? Do I deserve to call the true God my God?" In asking those questions, it is essential to remember several apparent paradoxes of God's Word. The first is that God reveals two equally true, but seemingly contradictory teachings in his Word: the law and the gospel. The law tells us what God expects of us. It commands certain things. It forbids others. It tells us what is pleasing to the holy and just God. It speaks a promise of life to those who obey, but it also thunders the threat of punishment for those who fail. What does the law say about us? Paul answers that question in Romans chapter 3. He tells us, "Now we know that whatever the law says, it says to those who are under the law, so that every mouth may be silenced and the whole world held accountable to God. Therefore no one will be declared righteous in God's sight by the works of the law; rather, through the law we become conscious of our sin" (verses 19,20). Did you notice what Paul says? The law makes the whole world accountable to God. In other words, when the law issues its threats, it applies to everyone. Why? How can God proclaim such a universally negative assessment of the entire human race? Paul helps us here too. A few chapters later, he says, "Just as sin entered the world through one man, and death through sin, and in this way death came to all people, because all sinned" (Romans 5:12). All sinned. All sinned because Adam, the first man, fell into sin and subsequently passed sin on to all his offspring, that is, to the entire human race. All humankind, regardless of background, are sinners, and so forever after the law always accuses every one of us. It exposes and uncovers our sin. It tells us because of that sin we deserve eternal separation from the holy God (Isaiah 59:2). Do I deserve to call the true God my God? The law proclaims the clear, unavoidable answer: No, I do not.

As universally true as that answer is, God has more to say. It's what we call the *gospel,* a word that means good news. In the gospel, God tells me that, though I do not deserve to belong to him, yet he has made just that possible. "He saw that there was no one, he was appalled that there was no one to intervene; so his own arm achieved salvation for him, and his own righteousness sustained him" (Isaiah 59:16). Yes, when no one could have done anything to save themselves or anyone else for that matter, God himself worked salvation. He saved us. He accomplished this greatest work through his dear Son, Jesus. Jesus came to this world. He lived a perfect life, the life God's righteous law prescribed. If that's not amazing enough, he did even more. He offered that life of perfection in place of a world full of sinners. He suffered the death on a cross that the world's sin had earned, the cruelest of deaths humanity in its evil has devised. In doing that, he paid the price of the world's sin. He took it away, and in its place, he gives us righteousness before God as his gift. Do I deserve to call the true God my God? No, I do not, but Jesus does deserve it, and he credits his righteousness to us. Through the Good News, God sends his Holy Spirit to work in our hearts, and there the Spirit works a miracle. He takes dead and lifeless hearts in the throes of sin and gives us new hearts, hearts that believe in Jesus and are alive. He gives us faith that trusts in God and looks to him for forgiveness and for every other good thing with the confidence that in Jesus he will grant all of them to us. No, I do not deserve to be a child of God, but by God's grace, that's what I am. Through faith in Jesus, that's what you are too.

That delight brings us to the second of the apparent paradoxes of God's Word: Because I am now a child of God, does that mean I am free from sin? On the one hand, the answer is yes. Paul assures us, "Now that you have been set free from sin and have become slaves of God, the benefit you reap leads to holiness, and the result is eternal life" (Romans 6:22). In Christ, we are free from sin. Christ has taken away its punishment. Christ has promised that its curse of death cannot touch us for all eternity. That means that even now, like Paul says, we live new lives no longer controlled by the sinful nature but lives of thanksgiving to God for all the good he has done for us. Scripture calls this the Christian life of sanctification.

But is our life of sanctification ever complete while we live on earth? Are we ever perfect in our Christian lives? Paul uses himself as the example to assure us the answer to that question is a decided no. Just one chapter later in Romans, he would say, "We know that the law is spiritual; but I am unspiritual, sold as a slave to sin. I do not understand what I do. For what I want to do I do not do, but what I hate I do. And if I do what I do not want to do, I agree that the law is good. As it is, it is no longer I myself who do it, but it is sin living in me. For I know that good itself does not dwell in me, that is, in my sinful nature. For I have the desire to do what is good, but I cannot carry it out. For I do not do the good I want to do, but the evil I do not want to do—this I keep on doing" (7:14-19). Though Paul had the new life of faith within him, he recognized the sinful nature still lurked within him and frustrated his efforts toward Christian sanctification.

God's Word compares it to a war. The sinful nature has entrenched itself within each of us. None of us can escape its reach because starting with Adam and Eve, the father and mother of all people, our parents have passed it on to each of us. But now we are in Christ. As members of Christ's body, the Holy Spirit has given us new life. In doing so, he drowned the sinful nature in the waters of Holy Baptism. He replaced our hearts of stone with hearts of flesh. In Christ, we delight to carry out God's commands and glorify him with our entire lives. God has already issued the final verdict. The final defeat of the sinful nature is certain, but still sin doesn't go down without a fight within each of us. No, though drowned, it learns to swim and continues to afflict us as long as earthly life endures. It fights against our new man of faith. It presses us with temptations. It haunts the thought and attitudes of our hearts with its evil desires. Though we are victorious children of God, we still contend with the sinful nature within us as long as this life endures, and the devil and this fallen world work together with that sinful nature to fight against our new man of faith. Paul speaks about this ongoing struggle in his letter to the Galatians. As he offers encouragement to live in the faith he says, "Walk by the Spirit, and you will not gratify the desires of the flesh. For the flesh desires what is contrary to the Spirit, and the Spirit what is contrary to the flesh. They are in conflict with each other, so that you are not to do whatever you want" (Galatians 5:16,17). Conflict is the nature of Christian living: the sinful nature battling against faith and vice versa. That's why God's Word can speak both about our sinful acts and our good works of faith. The Christian has both.

Consider what these apparent paradoxes mean for our faith itself. In light of what God's Word reveals about us, we recognize our faith is both perfect and imperfect. It is perfect in the sense that it is a flawless gift of God's Spirit which he placed in our hearts. It is perfect in the sense that it means we are recipients of all the gifts God grants through faith, namely, forgiveness of sin, the promise of eternal life, and peace with God. In the assurance we have through faith, we can say that it is perfect, but on the other hand, when it comes to faith's actual practice in our hearts and lives, then we must confess it is imperfect. We don't trust perfectly. Sometimes we doubt. We don't always look to God to provide for our every need. Sometimes we worry and complain. We don't always hold to God's power with the confidence that nothing is too hard for him. Sometimes we think his arm is too short to help us with our problem.

Why is that? Our living of our faith is imperfect because we still struggle under the weight of sin. Our faith coexists with this sinful nature. So when we speak of faith as it relates to our Christian lives, we recognize that faith can be strong or it can be weak. Faith can be large or small. Faith can have great confidence, or it can be wavering with doubt. In fact, we can say with certainty that doubts will assault faith because that is what sin within us will do by nature. To some, the Holy Spirit may give the gift of an especially strong faith that stands up better under pressure and avoids more doubting. To others, doubting will be a powerful temptation that the devil recognizes he can use as a particularly effective weapon.

We acknowledge we will all have doubts when it comes to our Christian faith. That doesn't mean we desire to have doubts or that we extol them as some kind of virtue. We don't want to think that our doubts somehow prove that our faith is genuine. No, we want to defeat doubts. We recognize that their existence testifies to our sin and our failure to fear, love, and trust God as we should.

Comfort in doubt

But God also extends his comfort in our doubts. Our doubts do not mean that our faith has failed. The anguish our doubts bring us is evidence of our faith fighting against the sinful nature. A dead man wouldn't pull his hand from a hot stove out of pain. No, it's the living man whose nerves tell him that the heat is harmful, and those nerves communicate that fact by sending painful signals that cause the man to cry out and pull his hand away as quickly as he can.

Likewise, were we dead in our sin, if we had no faith, unbelief wouldn't bother us at all. That would be our natural state. But instead, God has made us alive through faith, and that faith means we now recognize our own frailty and failings. It means we recognize our doubts.

In those moments, God doesn't thunder down his condemnation (though he would certainly be justified in doing so). Instead, he speaks to us with tenderness and mercy. As the prophet Isaiah describes the Lord, he says, "A bruised reed he will not break, and a smoldering wick he will not snuff out" (Isaiah 42:3). The Lord doesn't cut us off from him for our doubts. It was he who created faith within us when we were helpless to do anything on our own, when we were dead in sin. So now, even if and when our faith only hangs by a thread, if and when it flickers with the faintest whimper of strength, he does not for that reason cast us away from his presence. No, as our tender and gentle Good Shepherd, he patiently lifts us up and strengthens us through the gracious promises of his Word. He restores our soul. He teaches us to rely not on ourselves and our own strength but on him.

Encouragement in doubt

Of course, Jesus challenges us too. He rebuked the disciples as they tossed and turned in the boat during a storm. Despite their skills as fishermen, they had no doubt they were facing a certain death and burial at the bottom of the Sea of Galilee. They did, however, doubt their Savior's love for them and his

69

power over all things. "Don't you care if we drown?" they asked him (Mark 4:38). Jesus dealt with their problem. He saved them from the power of the storm, but then he also chastised his fearful disciples. They should have known better. They should have trusted Jesus. But in the moment of difficulty, they instead trusted earthly thoughts and what they thought was common sense. They didn't think anything could save them, so Jesus had what would certainly have been difficult words for them to hear. "Why are you so afraid? Do you still have no faith?" (Mark 4:40).

Don't we all need to hear those words of rebuke from time to time? In our weakness, we rely on the correction of God's Word to expose our faithless thoughts and actions. We need the correction that Jesus' questions to his disciples bring. We need it so that we can once again repent of our sin, look to Jesus for his promised forgiveness, and renew our strength to do better the next time. And no matter how much we grow in our faith during our earthly lives, we will always need that encouragement from the Word day in and day out.

But consider too that Jesus didn't abandon his disciples for their lack of faith. Just the opposite, he did just as they asked him (though their prayer was less than a shining example of strong faith). He calmed the storm and saved them from the depths. Don't ever doubt that Jesus does the same for you. In spite of the fact that our faith is imperfect, in spite of the fact that we often approach him with less than the confidence a dear child of God can have in going to his or her Father in prayer, still Jesus doesn't snuff out our faith or break the bruised reed of our trust in him. He gently encourages and restores and lifts us up.

A man stood in anguish at the thought of his little boy suffering. He wanted to have hope, but after so many failures, he just wasn't sure anyone could do anything. Against such a powerful enemy as that demon who had invaded his little boy's frame, he just didn't know whom or what he could trust. He wasn't even sure Jesus could do anything. But in that anguished moment, that man had a remarkable prayer, one we can emulate in our own lives. He prayed, "I do believe; help me overcome my unbelief!" (Mark 9:24). The man believed in Jesus. Still, he recognized the deficiency within himself, the failure to believe as he should have. He looked to his gracious Savior to fill what was lacking within him.

In those words we find an excellent model for us to follow in our own lives of faith. God is the one who has given us faith in him in the first place. He is the one who created what is pleasing to him within us. He did that through Word and sacrament. And so, he is also the one to whom we turn in our moments of weakness.

Our faith is far from perfect. The Lord knows this. He is the one who loved us in spite of our failure to carry out his commands. He is the one who loved us enough to give us faith in him when we were hostile to him (Romans 8:7). Like a loving Father, he is also patient with us in our doubts and weaknesses. He is the one—the only one—who can provide us with strength to grow and overcome our doubts.

As you continue the steps of your Christian pilgrimage, learn the prayer of that man begging Jesus for help. "Help me overcome my unbelief." Don't give in to the devil's deception that tempts you to believe that because you have doubts you don't have genuine faith. Instead, turn to the one who blessed you with your faith in the first place to give you forgiveness for your weakness and to supply whatever is lacking within you. God promises to grant rich supply to fill our needs both physical and spiritual. To the Philippians Paul offered the assurance, "My God will meet all your needs according to the riches of his glory in Christ Jesus" (4:19).

Yes, in our moments of struggle we can remember that ultimately it is God who began the good work of faith within us, and he is the one in whom we can have confidence to complete it. Consider Paul's closing words to the Thessalonians: "May God himself, the God of peace, sanctify you through and through. May your whole spirit, soul and body be kept blameless at the coming of our Lord Jesus Christ. The one who calls you is faithful, and he will do it" (1 Thessalonians 5:23,24). Paul's prayer is that God would bless and keep the Thessalonians, and his confidence and theirs was that their faithful God would bring his good work to completion. God would do it.

Ask the Lord to do the same for you, especially when you feel the weight of doubts. The Lord promises not to let you down. "This is the confidence we have in approaching God," his apostle John tells us, "that if we ask anything according to his will, he hears us" (1 John 5:14). Yes, it is the Lord's will to keep and strengthen you in the faith, and so when we ask him to do this, we know he delights to answer us with an unconditional yes.

Yes, in the one who gives us faith in the first place, we see unconditional grace again and again. A man came to Jesus with no hope. Could anyone do anything to help his son, his beloved son who was enduring an unimaginable torture? Yes, someone could. In spite of this father's uncertainty, in spite of his doubts about what Jesus could do, Jesus could do something. He could provide complete and perfect healing, and not only could he, but he did. With his almighty Word, Jesus provided exactly what that man was seeking. "I command you," Jesus said to the demon, "come out of him and never enter him again" (Mark 9:25). The demon had no choice but to obey. The one who called all things into being with his all-powerful Word speaks, and everything in heaven and on earth must obey. The demon came out, with the knowledge it could never enter the boy again because Jesus said so.

Despite that man's doubt, Jesus didn't skimp in providing him with divine help. Jesus didn't withhold his love and care from the man. Trust that Jesus does the same for you. As wavering as our faith sometimes can be, his love and care for us are unwavering. He promises that nothing can snatch us from his hand. Even "if we are faithless, he remains faithful, for he cannot disown himself" (2 Timothy 2:13). When the winds and waves of doubt batter you, don't look to yourself for strength. Look to Jesus. He won't let you down. ♥

8

I Know That
My Faith Struggles
Against Sin

Two men faced a difficult choice. Their particular circum-stances might have looked somewhat different to the outside observer but, still, they had much in common.

The first man was considering betraying a friend. Few would have any respect for someone who would do something like that, especially with a friend like this man had. The upside, however, was money, and this man had a heart for money. He just couldn't say no to it, even when it meant stealing from his friends and now even betraying one who was a friend and more.

The second man had made a bold claim. He promised he would never betray this same friend. In fact, he would rather die with this friend than turn his back on him.

In the end, the first man succumbed to temptation. He betrayed his friend, and things couldn't have gone any worse for that friend. As a result of the first man's betrayal, his friend was arrested, charged with a capital crime, and was therefore at great risk of losing his life.

That made the second man's choice difficult. It was one thing to boldly proclaim allegiance to his friend while in safety. It was another to stand by him when he was at risk of losing his life, when associating with that friend put that man in danger, when standing by someone could lead to a horrible death.

"Aren't you one of them?" came the question. "Surely you were with him," came the accusation. And the second man panicked. "Know him? Of course I don't know him! It's silly, preposterous to think so!" So set on convincing the observers around him that he didn't know the accused (his friend) he called down curses, denying his acquaintance with his friend, now a condemned criminal.

The two men—Judas Iscariot and Simon Peter—faced a difficult choice, and they both made the same decision. They betrayed their friend, who of course was Jesus, the man who was not only their friend but also their teacher and their Savior.

It's shocking to consider. These men were two of Jesus' twelve disciples. He had handpicked them for service to him and his church. He had called them to follow him. They had learned from Jesus' teaching. They had benefited from private instruction and explanation that he didn't offer to the large crowds. The disciples followed Jesus from day to day and could learn from his example too. For three years they received the greatest spiritual training one could ever receive from the Lord of heaven and earth himself.

And that wasn't all! All this training they had received was to equip them so that they could be Jesus' chosen apostles, men sent out to be fishers of men for the kingdom of God. Their life's calling would be to proclaim the good news about Jesus to the world.

But nevertheless here they were, on the night before Jesus' death, and they seemed like anything but faithful followers of the Savior. Here they were betraying Jesus into the hands of his enemies—for money no less—and denying acquaintance with him—for personal safety no less—by calling down oaths. What could cause such a reversal?

Like a roaring lion

There are several lessons in the troubling accounts of Peter and Judas. One is that no one is ever above the danger of falling away. Sin is a pernicious and persistent enemy, and just because we might perceive ourselves or someone else to be strong in faith does not mean that sin is going to sit idly by and let someone glide through this life untroubled. Let no one, therefore, ever imagine him or herself to be too strong in faith to fall away. That can be a deadly spiritual error.

The second lesson follows closely from the first. The Lord wants us to be on our guard. He wants us to be on our guard because the enemies of our faith are going to bring their attacks. Through his apostle Peter, he tells us, "Be alert and of sober mind. Your enemy the devil prowls around like a roaring lion looking for someone to devour. Resist him, standing firm in the faith, because you know that the family of believers throughout the world is undergoing the same kind of sufferings" (1 Peter 5:8,9).

Sometimes the attacks will be obvious. Other times, they will be more subtle. Either way, however, we do well to recognize that God has given us a great treasure in faith, and that great treasure is in danger in this world.

The apostle Paul put it clearly and concisely when he warned the Corinthians, "So, if you think you are standing firm, be careful that you don't fall!" (1 Corinthians 10:12). The worst condition to find oneself in when sin and the devil attack is to be unprepared. Just as no military general would want to face an assault when his troops were asleep in the barracks, so we do not want to face our spiritual enemies in a state of spiritual drowsiness or unconsciousness. We are tempted to that condition when we don't believe we have anything to fear, when we believe our faith is secure or when we downplay what our spiritual enemies can do to harm us—when we think we are standing firm. That makes our attackers' work all the easier.

That's why we always want to be awake and prepared. We want to be fully conscious of the fact that attacks will confront us in this world so that when they do, we are ready for the battle. God's Word not only encourages us always to be spiritually awake and ready, but it tells us how to do that too. "Let the message of Christ dwell among you richly," the Lord tells us (Colossians 3:16). That's so important because Christ's Word is the double-edged sword that equips us to stand firm in the face of trial and temptation. A life immersed in God's Word Word, then, is key to the battle. That will make regular hearing of God's Word in public worship a priority. There not only do we hear God's Word, but we receive his Sacrament, which is a visible, tangible proclamation of that same gospel that builds us up in our faith. It will also mean personal time in God's Word in devotion and study. It will mean devoting time to studying God's Word in group settings with other Christians. Never before in human history has God granted his people so many opportunities to hear and study his Word. All that remains is for his people to seize those opportunities, to take up the weapons God gives us for the spiritual battle that is a guarantee as long as we live in this world (Ephesians 6:10-20).

God also teaches us to pray, to pray continually in fact (1 Thessalonians 5:17). We pray not only because God commands us to do so but because he promises to hear and answer our prayers. As we pray, we remember that Jesus taught us in his own prayer to ask primarily for the spiritual blessings that our God tells us he wants to impart to us. Those good things God grants will further equip us in our fight against our spiritual enemies and shield his precious gift of faith from attack.

The devil is clever in his attacks. Since he tempted Adam and Eve in the Garden of Eden, he has been busy tempting people to turn away from the living God in favor of his lies. With those lies, he condemns people to the eternal death he suffers for his own rebellion against God. As Jesus himself said, the devil has been a murderer from the beginning (John 8:44).

One of the devil's most effective strategies of attack, it seems, especially in an age that has ready and constant access to the gospel message, is to convince believers that they really don't need the gospel in their lives. Sadly, Christians today witness the effectiveness of that attack again and again. Young people depart from the promises they make at their confirmation. Though they may have spent ample time in God's Word during their youth, they walk away from it as they mature. Sometimes, all the activities of high school and college distract them and take away what in the past was time devoted to God's Word. Other times, the ungodly ideas of this world tempt them to despise the Word they learned as children and, as a result, lead them away from hearing it. In both cases, the devil has succeeded in depriving these young people of the weapon they need to fight the attacks he and the world will be sure to level against them. How terrible this is, especially when they are bound to experience more and greater temptations as they are beginning life on their own away from the safety and nurture of their parents.

But neither should we imagine that the devil limits this attack to young people. Any time he can convince people they don't need God's Word as a regular part of their lives, he succeeds in exposing believers' faith to his attacks. So often, he simply takes advantage of spiritual laziness and apathy. A slip here and there can turn into a pernicious habit. A believer was accustomed to regular time in God's Word, but neglecting worship here and there turns into missing more often than attending. Perhaps before the individual even realizes it, time in God's Word has become a thing of the past. The devil has succeeded in making one of God's people vulnerable to his attack.

Other attacks of the devil are more obvious. Sometimes he entices with the pleasures of this world. He tells the lie that the temporary "good" of this world outweighs the eternal good of faithfulness to God's Word. Money, sex, power—these are powerful temptations because the fallen human nature's desire to have them is insatiable. When the devil can convince someone that obtaining these things in ways that ignore God's Word is preferable, when he can convince believers to act on their wicked desires, he has succeeded in leading them into a path that is destructive to faith, that if left unchecked and uncorrected will eventually destroy it altogether.

Weakness versus unbelief

Sin, by its very nature, is opposed to faith. Sin grieves the Holy Spirit who gives us faith and who dwells in us through faith (Ephesians 4:30). At the same time, however, we recognize that none of us are free from sin. The apostle Paul lamented this fact as he considered his own life. He recognized the sin that was within him and so often reared its ugly head. In his letter to the Romans he says, "We know that the law is spiritual; but I am unspiritual, sold as a slave to sin. I do not understand what I do. For what I want to do I do not do, but what I hate I do. And if I do what I do not want to do, I agree that the law is good. As it is, it is no longer I myself who do it, but it is sin living in me. For I know that good itself does not dwell in me, that is, in my sinful nature. For I have the desire to do what is good, but I cannot carry it out" (7:14-18). Yes, even as we bask in God's gift of faith, each of us also laments the fact that we carry with us a sinful nature that so often displays itself in our thoughts, words, and actions.

Paul further explains the nature of the believer in his letter to the Galatians. There he says, "Walk by the Spirit, and you will not gratify the desires of the flesh. For the flesh desires what is contrary to the Spirit, and the Spirit what is contrary to the flesh. They are in conflict with each other, so that you are not to do whatever you want" (5:16,17). Every believer has faith. At the same time, however, every believer on earth still struggles against the inborn sinful nature, which produces sins in our thoughts, our words, and our actions. We can rightly say, therefore, that we are both saint (one of God's perfect and holy people) and sinner (one who transgresses God's holy will) all at the same time. Only when God takes us to heaven, either through our physical death on this earth or on the Last Day, will he free us completely from our sinful nature. Until then we believers will contend with falls into sin.

But doesn't sin separate us from God? Doesn't our sin imply that we do not have the Holy Spirit or faith? There are times when pondering questions like that might make us afraid, especially when we ponder the pervasiveness of sin in our lives or when we've fallen into a particularly troublesome or serious sin. Or what about the sinful habit that in spite of our best efforts we just can't seem to break?

In moments of turmoil like that, God's Word that he shares with us through the apostle Paul brings us comfort. Yes, we are sinful. Yes, we fall into sin every day, every hour, almost every moment! Yet God tells us there is no condemnation for those who are in Christ Jesus (Romans 8:1). God in his grace forgives our sins of weakness every moment of every hour. As far as the east is from the west, he has removed them from us (Psalm 103:12). In Jesus' blood, God has washed us clean, even though we continue to fall into sin. Whenever our sins trouble us, this good news brings our hearts great joy.

When our sin does not trouble us, on the other hand, then we are wise to recognize that we are on dangerous ground. Not only does sin grieve the Holy Spirit, but our hard-heartedness is good evidence that our faith has grown weak or, worse, is is altogether dead. Unrepentant, hardened sin is incompatible with a heart of faith. "What shall we say, then? Shall we go on sinning so that grace may increase?" (Romans 6:1). At the beginning of this chapter of Romans, Paul is asking a rhetorical question. When human nature considers the gospel, it may ask a question, "Well, if Jesus has taken away my sins, why not go on sinning? Enjoy life! Jesus has taken away all the guilt anyways!" Paul explains that such a view is incompatible with faith. He answers his own question: "By no means!" (Romans 6:2).

When someone gives into the devil's attacks to the point that sin is no longer a concern, then a line has been crossed. No longer is such a person a believer. Instead, someone who repeatedly and willfully sins, fully knowing the sin is contrary to God's will, and he is not concerned about it, has chased away the Holy Spirit and has lost faith.

The issue is one of attitude. When we feel our sin and are troubled by it, then we have God's promise that in Jesus nothing can separate us from the love of God. When we treat sin lightly however, God warns us, "Be careful that you don't fall!" (1 Corinthians 10:12). When we take sin lightly, when we are willing to live in that sin without turning from it in repentance, then we demonstrate we are in a dark spiritual place.

Yes, we would do well to be aware of the spiritual danger we are in every day of our lives. "I walk in danger all the way," the famous hymn tells us. That's because the devil is a subtle enemy. A lion on the savannah does not advertise to its prey that it is going to attack. Instead, it lurks under the cover of the tall grass. It takes advantage of the camouflage God has given it. Only when the prey wanders too close, when it's not alert to its surroundings does the lion pounce with claws extended and teeth bared.

"Did God really say?" The devil's first temptation in the Garden of Eden had the appearance of an innocuous question. The devil was just looking for clarification. He was inquiring about exactly what God had communicated to Adam and Eve. Lurking beneath the question, however, was an ugly truth. The devil under the guise of innocence was setting a trap. His aim was to lead Adam and Eve into sin and thus rebellion against their Creator. His questioning led to his lie, "You will not surely die!" and in no time Adam and Eve had plunged themselves into spiritual death, as they no longer trusted their Creator and his Word, as they put themselves in league with God's enemy in order to gain knowledge God had not given them, as they had separated themselves from God.

It's worth keeping in mind that Adam and Eve had the ability to say no to the devil's temptations. They were not born in sin, as all of humanity has been ever since (Romans 5:12). That means we, as fallen human beings, are all the more susceptible to the devil's temptations. We have to contend with a sinful nature that wants to agree with the devil and give in to his demands.

That makes it all the more critical that we put ourselves on guard against these daily temptations. The book of Proverbs tells us, "Above all else, guard your heart, for everything you do flows from it" (4:23). Yes, the temptations are all around us and within us. Their aim is to drive us from the faith God has given us.

As we consider the preciousness of our faith, what will we do in response to the danger of temptation? For one, we dare not ignore the danger or pretend like it's no big deal. Things we might consider minor or insignificant transgressions the devil can use to gain a foothold in our lives (Ephesians 4:27). While we might think such slips will have no effect in our lives, the devil will not rest with a foothold. No, he will use it to gain an even greater stranglehold in our lives. He will use it to consume and destroy us, if we allow it.

In the moments that the temptations you're facing seem too great to bear, don't trust in your own strength. Instead, find the strength you need to move forward in your faith in the Lord. "The joy of the LORD is your strength," Nehemiah says (8:10). He will give you everything you need to face the temptations this life brings. Yes, we do well to go to God for strength to help us in our time of need. He is faithful, and he will never let those temptations become more than he knows we can bear with his powerful help and aid (1 Corinthians 10:13).

We also don't go looking for temptation, nor do we put ourselves in situations where temptations are likely to afflict us. Consider Joseph. He not only avoided temptation when it came his way; he ran away from it (Genesis 39:10-12). In a similar way, consider seriously how temptation can affect your faith and avoid it whenever possible.

In this sinful world, pure avoidance will not always be possible. "Things that cause people to stumble are bound to come," Jesus told his disciples (Luke 17:1). Yes, each of us will face temptations. That is the reality of life in this world.

But the Lord also promises that as powerful as the devil is, he is no match for our Savior. With Jesus by our side, we have nothing to fear. "Resist the devil, and he will flee from you," the Lord promises us (James 4:7). Think of it! The devil who has been around since the time of Adam and Eve, who has been at work tempting people throughout the ages, will actually flee from us. Armed with the double-edged sword of God's Word, accompanied by our ever-present Savior, the devil cannot stand against us.

In his famous hymn, "A Mighty Fortress Is Our God," Martin Luther said about our foe, the devil: "One little word can fell him." The little word Luther probably had in mind was "liar." That's what the devil is, and when he speaks to us, that's all that he will tell us. With that little word, therefore, we expose the devil for what he is and we make him powerless over us. ♥

9

I Know That
My Faith Will Know Fully

They had waited for years. Waiting is not something our human nature does well or is eager to do. Often in our society of instant gratification, we grow impatient at the prospect of waiting only a few moments for anyone or anything. Two people Scripture tells us about from the early life of Jesus, however, waited far longer than that.

By the time we meet them, we get the distinct impression both of them had been waiting for a long time. One, we're told, had been waiting for decades. After her husband had died after only a brief marriage, she had spent the remainder of her life in the house of the Lord. There she worshiped day and night, filling her days with fasting and praying. When we meet her, she was already 84 years old.

Scripture doesn't provide us quite as many details about the other patient individual. Nonetheless, we have several reasons to think he too had spent years waiting. The gospel writer Luke tells us that this man was waiting for the consolation of Israel. As a special grace to him, the Holy Spirit had revealed that he would not die before he could lay eyes on the Anointed One who would redeem God's people. When God at last brought that promise to fulfillment and allowed him to see the baby Jesus in the temple, this man named Simeon praised God by saying that he, as a result of God fulfilling his promise to him, was now ready to depart this life. "Sovereign Lord, as you have promised, you may now dismiss your servant in peace" (Luke 2:29).

That other individual, a prophetess named Anna, during the Christmas season also gave thanks to God for giving her the privilege of bringing fulfillment to her faith. She "spoke about the child to all who were looking forward to the redemption of Jerusalem" (Luke 2:38).

We often give special attention to the story of Simeon and Anna. What a blessing God gave to them in permitting these aged believers the opportunity to see the Savior during their lifetime.

These people of God are symbolic of the entire Old Testament church. Through long ages past, the church looked forward with eager expectation to the time when God would at last fulfill the promise of sending his Anointed One: the promise that came first to Adam and Eve, to Abraham, Isaac, and Jacob, to King David, the promise that God clarified and sharpened through Isaiah and Jeremiah, the long-promised hope of God's people. For ages, believers looked ahead and asked, "Is it time yet?" At last, Simeon and Anna in the sunset of their lives had the privilege of seeing the promise fulfilled.

"Sovereign Lord, as you have promised, you may now dismiss your servant in peace. For my eyes have seen your salvation, which you prepared in the sight of all nations: a light for revelation to the Gentiles, and the glory of your people Israel" (Luke 2:29-32). For Simeon, it was enough to see Immanuel in the flesh. No, he didn't get to see Jesus some three decades later bring his redemptive work to completion. He didn't even get to see the miracles or hear Jesus' teaching of authority, nor did he see Jesus proclaim his work finished on the cross or rise from the dead three days later. Holding in his aging arms that little infant who was God's Son in the flesh was enough.

Looking forward

It's certainly fitting that the church continues to sing Simeon's song. How fitting that many of our opportunities for worship conclude with these words. In worship we get to see God's salvation. He reveals it to us as he himself is present with us in Word and sacrament. He speaks to each one of us and announces our forgiveness through the words of absolution. He puts into our mouths his body and blood as a seal of his love and forgiveness. Like Simeon, we have seen the salvation that God has prepared as a light for us and all nations.

In another way, we are like Simeon. Like him, we have seen our faith fulfilled many times over. Especially as we consider our Old Testament brothers and sisters, we see the truth in that statement. They had only God's promises about Jesus. They didn't have the benefit of seeing Jesus fulfill all those promises perfectly. They didn't have the blessing of looking back and seeing in wonderful detail how God won our salvation. They had to look ahead with hope and trust in God.

At the same time, God still leaves room for faith for us too. Like Simeon, we have not seen all of God's promises fulfilled just yet. We still await our final redemption from this present evil age. Not yet do we behold with our eyes the Lord Jesus in all his glory as our eternal King. For that, we, like Simeon, must wait. Like Simeon, we are in the age of *now but not yet*. We have seen God's salvation. Soon, we shall see it even more clearly.

So, like Simeon, we wait. We look forward to the final fulfillment of God's gracious promises, and as we do so, it's not always easy. As long as this life endures, we are not yet home. Instead we sojourn on this earth as temporary residents.

What's more, this earth is like that wilderness through which Moses and the Israelites wandered for 40 years, full of troubles and temptations. Ever since Adam and Eve's fall, this world has groaned under the weight of sin. As temporary residents of this earth, we too feel that weight. The burdens of life in this world are living proof of it. The devil, the world, and our own flesh weigh us down.

That means our faith on this earth will always remain imperfect, a work in progress. Contrary to this imperfectness, the rewards God promises to our faith are a guarantee. Forgiveness, life, and salvation are our sure inheritance because God does not award these gifts on the basis of our faith's virtue. Instead he awards them as a gift of grace on account of Christ's perfect life in our place. Faith great and small receives these certain blessings as a gift of God.

Our faith as a fruit of the Holy Spirit, however, will always remain imperfect during our wandering through the wilderness of this world. We will struggle with doubts. We will waver in times of uncertainty. We will fall into temptation. Our faith will remain imperfect.

So often we might wish God would just put an end to the struggle once and for all. "Why can't God prove everything he says so that we no longer have to rely on faith in things unseen? Why can't he make it easier to believe in him?" "Why can't he just give his believers a life of charm and ease right now instead of down the road in heaven?" At some point or another, especially in times of testing, many believers can struggle with such thoughts, much like Simeon and Anna must have during their many years of waiting for the time when God would finally reveal his salvation to them.

In the meanwhile, God does not leave us without encouragement. He gives his Word. God's Word serves to help us in those moments when we feel weak. "Everything that was written in the past was written to teach us, so that through the endurance taught in the Scriptures and the encouragement they provide we might have hope" (Romans 15:4). Yes, just like an encouraging word from a trusted friend can help us through earthly difficulties, so God's encouraging Word reminds us of what awaits us at this life's conclusion.

God also assures us that while we might perceive God as being slow to keep his promises, that is not the case. "The Lord is not slow in keeping his promise, as some understand slowness. Instead he is patient with you, not wanting anyone to perish, but everyone to come to repentance" (2 Peter 3:9). To you and me, it might seem like some two thousand years is a long time to wait for Jesus' return. It might seem like perhaps God has forgotten about his promises or that he wasn't serious about them in the first place. Indeed, many doubters use the millennia that have gone by since Jesus' return to heaven as an excuse for rejecting God's promise (2 Peter 3:3,4).

As believers, however, we want to remember that the Lord does not reckon time as we do. "With the Lord a day is like a thousand years, and a thousand years are like a day" (2 Peter 3:8). As the Creator of time, God is above time. It does not come and go as it does for us who are bound by it. Because we perceive thousands of years going by as a long time does not mean that God has somehow forgotten what he has spoken. Regardless of the passage of time or how our limited human reason perceives it, he will bring his promises to completion.

God, however, does not promise to do so on our timeline. He does not promise to reveal the truth underlying all his promises while we dwell on this earth. Instead, it pleases him to continue to save his people through what seems as foolishness to the world. He delights for his people to have faith in him, even though our sinful nature and our sinful environment will mean that faith is always under attack and always imperfect. It pleases him for his people to practice faith when it is not always easy to do so; yes, when our reason tells us that it is in vain.

So we do well to exercise patience. Like faithful Abraham, like faithful Simeon and Anna, like Moses who faithfully led God's people in the wilderness for all those years, so you too wait for the Lord. "Wait for the LORD; be strong and take heart and wait for the LORD" (Psalm 27:14). In the moments that it seems like you can't go on any longer, in the moments when you feel yourself sinking down, turn to the Lord. He will give you the strength you need. Remember that his promises are sure and take heart. Remember that your faith is in the always-faithful God who will bring his Word to completion. Nothing in all creation is more certain.

Then I shall know fully

God will not leave our faith imperfect forever. The time is coming soon, the Lord tells us, when he will pull back the curtain so that the truth will be plain to everyone. Jesus will return. It's true that no one knows when that blessed day will occur. No one can predict it or tell us when it will be. It may be hours away. It may be centuries or even millennia away, but the fact remains, Jesus is coming back. At that time, everyone will see for themselves the truth that Scripture has been proclaiming all along. Everyone will confess that Jesus is Lord, that he came to this earth to save the world from its sin. Those with faith in him will confess this with delight and rejoice with singing as they live with him forever in heaven. Those who rejected Jesus will confess the same truth to their everlasting shame and contempt as they suffer the punishment for their sin for all eternity. In the end, every knee will bow and every tongue confess that Jesus Christ is Lord to the glory of God the Father (Philippians 2:10,11).

When that day comes (or when the Lord calls us as individuals to heaven through death), our faith will no longer have the struggles with which we are so accustomed in this present evil age. No longer will we have doubts. No longer will our faith waver. No longer will we be subject to the devil's or the world's temptations. Our faith will no longer be in things unseen. It will no longer be certainty in what is hoped for, because we will take hold of the prize of our faith. Our faith will find its eternal fulfillment.

With eager anticipation, the apostle Paul looked forward to that time. He shared the joy of it with the Corinthians when he wrote, "Now we see only a reflection as in a mirror; then we shall see face to face. Now I know in part; then I shall know fully, even as I am fully known" (1 Corinthians 13:12).

Isn't that a delightful picture of our faith in Christ? During our time on this earth, we must acknowledge that our faith is far from perfect. We can only see a poor reflection, like looking in a broken or foggy mirror. A broken mirror might allow us to see basic shapes. It might allow us to get a general picture of what we're looking at, but it remains far from the kind of perfect sight we get from looking at the thing itself in broad daylight. The same is true with our faith. We can know the truth. In fact, God in his grace has revealed a great amount that we can know, but one day we will know far more. On this earth we cannot make out and understand every fine detail about the truth. We wish we knew more and could understand more. How often as we examine our own faith must we confess that Paul's description is so true. Our faith falls short. Though we confess our failing, we can also rejoice because we know that will not always be the case.

Yes, the time is coming when Christ will come again. At that time, our faith will change. Its knowledge will be perfect. Its trust will be complete. We will know fully. Just as God has known us perfectly all along, just as he does while we wander through this earth, there will come a time when he will bless our faith with the completeness we now can only earnestly desire. We will know as God has known us in the perfection of fellowship with him.

Despite his faithful leadership of God's people, Moses' knowledge of the earthly Promised Land never extended beyond the ability to look at it from afar. He did not have the privilege of settling down in it and enjoying rest from all the Israelites' wandering. He did, however, have the joy of entering the Promised Land of heaven. There, together with Simeon and Anna who centuries later got to see the beginning of Jesus' ministry, God freed him from all the burdens of this imperfect world, and he gave him the complete and perfect faith Paul described in Corinthians.

That same hope is ours. One day soon we will be with Moses and Simeon and Anna and all believers from throughout the ages. When the burdens of life weigh you down, when you feel like your faith is ready to topple under the weight of everything you're enduring in this life, then keep your eyes on the prize. Remember, the time is coming when the Lord will give you the perfect faith of life eternal in heaven. Either he will call you to his side or he will return on the clouds with all of his angels. Either way, your faith will be free of all its present troubles forever and ever.

So as you contemplate your faith through this walk of life, as you ask how you can be sure of your faith, and how you can recognize it and make sure you are appropriately caring for it, do so always with an eye on the goal of heaven.

Paul gave us the encouragement, "Run in such a way as to get the prize" (1 Corinthians 9:24). The one who runs to get the prize doesn't allow other things to distract, things like the crowd and its cheers, what might be going on around the race course, or what the other runners might be doing. No, the one running for the prize has a singular focus. That focus is the finish line and the prize that awaits the one who crosses it first.

That is exactly how the Lord wants us to view life. Of course, we have many things that confront us in life. God gives to us a variety of responsibilities and ways to serve him, but we want none of that to distract us from the final prize of our faith. We want to keep our eyes fixed on the heavenly prize that Jesus has won for us. We don't have to run like runners in a race with the nervous trepidation that if someone else crosses first we are going to miss out. No, Jesus has already guaranteed us the victory. All that remains is for us to run the race marked out for us with the confidence that the victory is ours.

A race is exciting. It's exciting as we consider crossing the finish line and the joy that comes from victory. Let nothing distract you from that. Let nothing take away from the joy that will certainly be yours in Christ. Your faith gives you that certainty, and so our faith also compels us to look forward with eagerness as we anticipate the second coming of Christ. In our hearts we pray, "Come, Lord Jesus." We pray that because we know that we know. ♥